# HOW TO MAKE MONEY WHILE YOU ARE SLEEPING

# PHOTOGRAPHY BOOKS
# BY RICK SAMMON

RICK SAMMON
AND THE ALL-STAR PHOTO COACHES

# HOW TO
# MAKE
# MONEY
# WHILE
# YOU ARE
# SLEEPING

A PHOTOGRAPHER'S
GUIDE TO PASSIVE INCOME
AND OTHER SAVVY BUSINESS STRATEGIES

Cover design by Ivica Jandrijevic
Interior layout and design by www.writingnights.org
Book preparation by Chad Robertson
Edited by Chad Robertson and Cindy Snyder

ISBN: 979-8-4986-4106-5
Library of Congress:
LIBRARY OF CONGRESS CATALOGING-IN-PUBLICATION DATA:
NAMES: Sammon, Rick, author
TITLE: How to Make Money While You are Sleeping – A Photographer's Guide to Passive Income – And Other Savvy Business Strategies
DESCRIPTION: Independently Published, 2020
IDENTIFIERS: ISBN 9798498641065 (Perfect bound)
SUBJECTS: | Non-Fiction | Photography |
Motivation | Inspiration | Passive Income | Business
CLASSIFICATION: Pending
LC record pending

Printed in the United States of America.
Printed on acid-free paper.

As with any book that deals with technology there is always a risk of making references to companies or technologies that have already ended up in the dustbins of history. Once-dominant brands of today can quickly be the forgotten brands of tomorrow. The author has kept the information as contemporary and up-to-date as possible up until the date of publication. However, the author recognizes that current internet giants could completely vanish from the online environment.

24   23   22   21   20   19   18   17   8   7   6   5   4   3   2   1

Dedicated to the memory of my dad, Robert M. Sammon, Sr., who, through his example, showed me the importance of paying careful attention to one's income, expenses, and investments ... as well as the benefit of living below your means.

My dad, an amateur photographer who got me started taking pictures, also gave me some invaluable advice when it comes to making money: "It takes a lot of peanuts to feed an elephant." In other words, he was saying that all those pennies and dollars can add up, which is the theme of this book.

*"If you don't find a way to make money while you sleep,*
*you will work until you die."*
—WARREN BUFFETT

# CONTENTS

# Acknowledgements
# & Networking

cknowledgments and networking? Why is Rick mixing these two topics together?" you may be asking. Chad Robertson, the producer of this book, may be asking the same question—because he strictly follows (with exceptions) the Chicago Manual of Style for producing books for his clients.

For two reasons:

1. Most people don't read the acknowledgments in a book, unless they expect to see their name listed. So, I added "Networking" as a teaser in the hope that you would not skip over this section. I want you to see who contributed to this work because I really could not have produced this book without their help—each and every one of them.

2. I wanted to jumpstart the learning process right away, by talking about the importance of networking, and leaven the lessons by way of my friends' experiences that they've given me permission to share.

Those friends—wonderful photographers who I refer to in this book as "The All-Star Photo Coaches"—offered to share their advice, stories, and experience with you simply because I asked. They feel, as I do, that we are all in this together. We help and support each other. As Ringo sings, "With a little help from my friends." And speaking of Ringo, the idea for "The All-Star Photo Coaches" was inspired by his band, Ringo Starr & His All-Starr Band.

Sure, my contributors may get (and I hope) an additional benefit out of participating in this work. They may get a new photo workshop or photo tour participant, a new newsletter or podcast subscriber, a new follower on Instagram, or they may sell a few books or get a few sign-ups for personal coaching sessions.

Are they in competition with me or with each other? Technically, yes. However, as funny as it may sound, we all feel as though we don't have any competition because, our friendship and the networking benefits outweigh that competitive feeling.

I can't stress the importance of networking enough. You can't do it alone. The more friends you have and the larger your network, the more successful you will be. I promise.

The opposite philosophy is conveyed by the famous Japanese motto: "Business is War." I can't promise you, but my guess is that if you follow this philosophy, you will lose the "war" of building your business.

If you can't network in person, say at live photo events, network—and become friends with—professional photographers online. It works. For example, I have never actually met three of the contributors for this book: Richard Bernabe, PhotoJoseph, and Tim Wallace. I followed them online, commented on their posts, shared their tweets and so on. They did the same. We became friends, and they gladly offered their contributions to this book.

I also network online through the **Photo Therapy Facebook Group** that I started in March of 2020 during the Covid-19 Pandemic. More on Facebook Groups in **Chapter 6: Start a Facebook Group**. For now, I can tell you that Facebook Groups can be a valuable marketing tool, as long as you keep them educational and fun, and don't use them for a hard sell. Our members and moderators will vouch for that, too.

Okay. Here is the full list of all-star photo coaches that I am proud to call my friends. I added a short description after each name to illustrate how I see them.

**Sean Bagshaw**—An awesome landscape photographer, a smart networker and respectful of older photographers.

**Larry Becker**—The best on-camera photo personality I know. And one of the nicest guys you will ever meet.

**Richard Bernabe**—At the top of his game in wildlife photography. A fun guy, even though he rarely smiles in photos.

**Scott Bourne**—A good bass player, and the person who told me to get into social media many years ago. Best bird photographer out there, too.

**Steve Brazill**—An awesome podcaster and great rock-star photographer. Steve is also a good writer, but, most importantly, a good dad.

**Ron Clifford**—A deeply caring and passionate photographer and speaker and the only guy I know who gave a TED talk.

**Skip Cohen**—An excellent businessperson who I have known since the early 1980s when he was the president of Hasselblad.

**Joel Grimes**—A master of fine-art portraiture, and the photographer who actually cracked the code of lighting.

**Mat Hayward**—Take stock in what Mat says. He is an awesome evangelist for stock photography.

**Karen Hutton**—A purveyor of awesomeness in all she does –photographically and beyond. Karen is an inspiration to all.

**Don Komarechka**—The "snowflake guy." The master of macro photography. He reminds me of myself when I was his age.

**Lewis Kemper**—A serious photographer, a good person, and one of the three people I know who was an assistant to Ansel Adams.

**Ibarionex Perello**—The best street photographer I know with the best podcasting voice. Someday I will learn how to pronounce his first name.

**Ian Plant**—Man-oh-man I wish I had Ian's energy, but then again,

I am old enough to be his father. A perfectionist in all that he does, from podcasting to landscape photography.

**PhotoJoseph**—One of the best examples of someone who uses social media to spread his message and to gain followers. I love the guy, even though I don't know his last name.

**Ant Pruitt**—The only pro who calls me, "Mr. Sammon." A great podcaster, friend, and most important, dad.

**Fernando Santos**—A moderator of the KelbyOne community who is beyond nice and beyond responsive and caring.

**Jonathan and Angela Scott**— My dear friends in Kenya are wildlife photographers extraordinaire. I tell people all the time, "I'd like to be more like Jonathan Scott," because he is a good photographer and a good person.

**Larry Tiefenbrunn**—The inventor of the Platypod and Platyball, and pretty good on vocals when we make music with his son on guitar and keyboards.

**Tim Wallace**—I've never met the dude in person, but he was kind enough to contribute to this book. He's also a top commercial photographer and one of my favorite KelbyOne instructors.

My best friend, wife, and excellent iPhone photographer Susan Sammon gets an über-thank you for her help with, well ... all I do. Susan manages the financial side of our business, which is beyond tremendously appreciated. If I do another book with the same word count as this one, I could write nearly 40,000 nice words about Susan Sammon, whose motto is: "If you have the opportunity to be right or kind, be kind."

Yet another friend who gets my thanks is Chad Robertson, top gun at WritingNights (www.writingnights.org). Chad produced this book, as well as *Photo Therapy, Photo Quest,* and *Photo Pursuit.* Chad, by the way, was introduced to me by another friend, Trey Ratcliff of Stuck in Customs (www.stuckincustom.com) fame.

My editor for this book, Cindy Snyder, was introduced to me by my friend Chris Main at KelbyOne and gets my thanks for all her hard work and dedication.

As you can see, networking is very important.

Before my final thank you, here's another very important tip about networking: Do not make enemies. Just one enemy can cause you loss of sales if they post negative comments about you on social media. An enemy can also get under your skin, causing you to have a lot of negative feelings.

I know all this because, early on in my career, I had two enemies who went out of their way to give me a hard time. I do take half the blame for the situation. And I learned my lesson. So again, do not make enemies.

One way to avoid making enemies is to curb your ego. If you need some help in that area or know someone who could use some advice, I recommend, reading/listening to *Ego is the Enemy* by Ryan Holiday. From the book's prologue: "While the history books are filled with tales of obsessive visionary geniuses who remade the world in their images with sheer, almost irrational force, I've found that history is also made by individuals who fought their egos at every turn, who eschewed the spotlight, and who put their higher goals above their desire for recognition."

Finally, thank you for being here! I hope you learn and earn from the advice on the following pages.

# Author's Preface

Hey! I know you love photography. As do I. I know you want to make beautiful pictures and have fun processing those pictures. As do I. I know photography is a very important part of your life. It's a very important part of mine. I know you want to share your photographs with others.

And I know something else. You are reading this book because you'd like to generate some extra income to help you pursue your passion—again, as do I.

After writing forty-two books (most richly illustrated with photographs) and having been a freelance photographer for more than thirty years, I thought I'd share my thoughts on the business side of being a photographer for a change. Lots of photographers come to me for advice on how to "make it" as a photographer.

On these pages you will find many **do's** on how to generate income while you are sleeping, as well as when you are awake.

Through specific examples, shared both by yours truly and by some of my successful photographer friends, you will learn how the expression, "The harder your work, the luckier you become," applies to generating passive income. Rephrasing that expression for this book: "The more time you put into generating passive income while you are awake, the more income you will generate while you are sleeping."

However, before we get to all those **do's**, here are two important **don'ts** to keep in mind:

1) Don't give up your day job to generate passive income ... at least not yet.
2) Don't put all your eggs in one basket.

I share this two don'ts because I don't want you to get the impression that making money while you are sleeping is the secret to making it as a photographer and to making it a full-time job. It's simply one of many methods that can help you supplement your income. As it turns out these methods are not only rewarding, they're also fun!

Rick Sammon
Croton on Hudson, New York
October 2021

# INTRODUCTION

*"Dad, you're not only a photographer, but you are also an entrepreneur who happens to be a photographer."*
—MARCO SAMMON

That's what my son Marco, seventeen years old at the time, said after I introduced myself as a photographer at a neighborhood party.

Marco, who has since received his PhD in Finance and who is currently an associate finance professor at Harvard Business School, was making the point that although I take pictures for a living, I spend a lot of time—the majority of my time actually—on the business side of my profession. I'm always working hard on new projects—writing books, setting up affiliate programs, cultivating sponsorships, recording online classes and podcasts, and so on.

Marco also observed that I spend a lot of time promoting those projects on social media, and then tracking the results. We'll talk more about tracking sales later in this book, but for now, if you self-publish a paperback or Kindle version on Amazon.com, you can actually track sales on an hourly basis—which I don't encourage because it can become addictive. However, I have to admit that I do track sales quite frequently when I release a new book.

So, the message here is this: as much as you love photography (as I do), and as much as you want to save the world (its people, wildlife, environment, and so on) with your craft, it's important to understand that in order to succeed you must also be a good businessperson—which involves generating income while you are both awake and asleep.

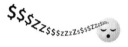

If you know me from some of my other photography books, photo workshops, tours, seminars, and online classes, you may be thinking, "I like Rick's photography and I've learned some cool things from him, but what could he possibly know about sound business practices?" Well, believe it or not, before becoming a professional photographer I spent ten years (1980–1990) at Bozell & Jacobs as vice president/group supervisor on the Minolta camera account. At that time Bozell & Jacobs was one of the largest advertising and public relations firms in the world.

At that agency I learned about the business side of photography, as well as how to promote Minolta photographers, including famed Beatles' photographer, Harry Benson.

When I left the agency, I had the "ammo" to promote myself through advertising and PR. I had also learned the business side of a professional photographer's life from working with other famous photographers like fashion photographer, Robert Farber, and United Nations photographer, John Isaac.

The lessons I learned at the agency were invaluable, as were the business lessons I learned as editor of *Studio Photography* magazine (from 1978 to 1980). Having been hired with no editorial experience, my boss and the publisher of the magazine, Rudy Maschke, said this to me when I asked him for my first raise: "Sammon, you are learning so much that you should be paying me."

On these pages I will share all I know about the business side of photography with you, which of course includes making money while you are sleeping.

These lessons have helped my wife, Susan, and I run our business for more than thirty years—and I can tell you, there is nothing like running your own business. As a small business owner, you learn very quickly that you are both the "chief cook and bottle washer," as my dad used to say.

When thinking of generating income while you are sleeping, please don't get me wrong, I still work my butt off during my waking hours—because I love what I do. And as the saying goes: "If you love what you do, you never need to work a day in your life."

Generating income while you are sleeping starts with your waking time, something we'll cover in the next chapter, **Before You Doze Off.**

If you are new to generating passive income, the cool thing is that after you put in the work, you can doze off (take a nap during the day or go off to bed) and wake up a little richer than you were before you closed your eyes.

The key phrase here is "a little." Before I explain, here's another expression my dad shared with me: "Everything is relative." In other words, "a little" means something different to different people. For example, "a little" passive income *each* day from different sources (including books, online classes, and crowdfunding projects) could possibly add up to a very nice source of income. In fact, I know several well-known photographers whose major source of income is generated passively.

In subsequent chapters, you'll see how you can generate "a little" income while you sleep with different money-making projects that you can create during your waking hours. These projects include:

- Affiliate programs
- Downloadable PDF eBooks
- Kindle eBooks
- Amazon paperback books
- Traditional books
- Audiobooks
- Online training classes
- Buy Me a Coffee
- Webinars
- Monetizing a YouTube channel
- Sponsorships
- Kickstarter/Crowdfunding projects
- Product development
- Online print sales
- Newsletters
- Podcasts

Dollarwise, you might be asking, "How much is 'a little?'" As I usually say when someone asks me these questions, the answer is, "It depends." It depends on the project/product, the selling price, how well your item sells, how well you promote it, your name, and the size of your audience.

About the size of your audience: you need to do "everything in your power," as Don Corleone said in the movie *The Godfather* to build and cultivate it. It's the key to success.

We will talk more about building your audience/followers later in this book, but for now, that includes being very active on social media, building your mailing list, and treating *everyone* who comes into your "store" (your website) with respect.

Let's take a *quick* look at just three of the aforementioned money-making projects. Keep in mind that this book was written in 2021 and things may have changed by the time you read this text.

I feel compelled to reiterate that this is only a quick look to illustrate that there is passive income to be made on the internet. We'll go into more detail later in this book.

**Affiliate Programs.** Basically, an affiliate or associate program is a system that lets you keep a very small percentage of a sale by posting a custom-for-you, company-generated link to a product. The more links you post—on social media, on your website, in newsletters, and so on—the more peanuts you make.

Sounds simple? It is, but there is more to it. I'll tell you all the nuts and bolts in **Chapter 4: The Advantage of Affiliate Programs**. You may be surprised at how the Amazon Associates Program works, and how you can sometimes generate income from products that you are not even promoting.

**Publishing Paperback and Kindle Books on Amazon.** First, let's talk about paperback books: KDP (Kindle Direct Publishing) offers a fixed 60% royalty rate on paperbacks sold via Amazon's various marketplaces.

When it comes to Kindle books (eBooks readable on any device), authors who self-publish on Amazon through KDP earn a 70% royalty on books priced between $2.99 and $9.99, and a 35% royalty on books that cost more or less than that.

If you offer a book on Amazon for $10, you'll receive $7 for each copy sold. Sell a few thousand copies (typical for a photo book by a well-known author), and that's a lot of peanuts.

As an author who has published four books (including this one) on Amazon, as well as dozens of paper books with traditional book publishers, I can tell you that Amazon offers a much higher royalty (70% compared to about 5% to 8% for traditional publishing). But Amazon does not offer advances, while a number of photo book publishers still do.

In addition, Amazon does not do foreign language translations, which, when done by traditional publishers, can generate added income. If you want to do a translated edition and post it on Amazon in different countries, a professional translation can cost upward of $2,000. On top of that, you need to start from scratch when it comes to the actual production of the book. If you can't DIY it, this can cost anywhere from $1,500 to $4,000.

**Online Classes on Training Sites:** Payment for online classes on established training sites, some of which have tens of thousands of members, varies from company to company and individual to individual (usually based on the instructor's popularity and social media following).

I've recorded thirty-six online classes with different training sites. KelbyOne (www.kelbyone.com), where I have recorded more than thirty photography and Photoshop classes, is my favorite and where I now publish exclusively.

As an aside, KelbyOne offers more than forty business classes. For the photography businessperson, these classes offer invaluable information.

While payment for an online class varies from site to site and company to company, the average class completion payment is between $1000 and $3000, and the royalty payment is a few dollars per class.

I'll go into more detail as to what goes into the production of an online class in **Chapter 11: Record an Online Class or Classes.** But for now, if an online training site has thousands of members and many watch your class—that's right, more peanuts.

We'll talk more about different make-money-while-you-are-sleeping projects on the following pages—starting with the next chapter, **Before You Doze Off.**

While you're reading that chapter, as well as the chapters that follow, I encourage you to keep the "snowball effect" in mind. A snowball starts out as a few snowflakes, and as it rolls down a hill, it gets larger and larger, until it eventually starts to melt. When you see sales "melting away," it's time for you to "wake up" and get back to work promoting your products.

In closing this Introduction, I'd like to emphasize the epigraph for this book: "If you don't find a way to make money while you sleep, you will work until you die." —Warren Buffett

I'll add to that a story from my friend and wonderful photographer Fernando Santos. "I have a friend" he says, "who, when someone told him how busy they were, the friend said, 'You're so busy working that you don't even have time to make money.'"

In other words, it's important to pay attention to your finances, especially your passive income.

# 1.

# BEFORE YOU DOZE OFF

*"Tired minds don't plan well. Sleep first, plan later."*
—WALTER REISCH

While you're reading this book, you're probably going to notice that I like quotes. Each chapter begins with a quote that I tried to match to the theme of that chapter.

This chapter is an exception. I'll begin with three well-known quotes. Each one applies to making money while you are sleeping, even though at first glance it may not seem that way. Take a look, and then I'll explain what I mean.

*"You snooze you lose."*

*"You must put in the time before you have the time."*

*"You have to spend money to make money."*

**"You snooze you lose."** Simply put, you need to spend your waking hours working—creating materials (online classes, books, prints, PDF downloads, etc.), setting up your passive income system (affiliate links, downloads, online ordering, and the other topics covered in this book), and then marketing your work, which I will cover in **Chapter 3: Socialize or Succumb.**

The more time you spend snoozing in the beginning of your quest to make money while you are sleeping, the more you will lose out on generating passive income.

**"You must put in the time before you have the time."** This is basically the same concept as "You snooze you lose." I include it here to reinforce the idea that hard work pays off … for years (and maybe even generations) to come. For example, I know authors who are still making money on books that were written decades ago. It's the same for online classes. And the same for old blog posts with affiliate links that folks stumble upon.

**"You have to spend money to make money."** There's an old expression, "Everyone needs an editor," which by the way, includes me.

You may need to hire an editor or proofreader to help you with a blog post, article, copy for a book (traditional, Amazon, or PDF), or an app. You may need to hire a camera person and editor to help you with an online video class. That money will be well spent because it will make you "look" better.

If you don't want to spend money, offer the person a percentage of sales. I do one or the other depending on the project.

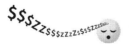

Speaking of time, like me, most of my professional photographer friends spend more time working on the business side of photography than they do taking pictures. My breakdown is about eighty to ninety percent business, and about ten to twenty percent actually making and processing pictures.

As a result of their efforts, most of my friends have a nice passive income, in addition to a nice active income.

I asked a few of these friends to share their business vs. photography ratio, along with their best business advice. Take a listen.

**Ian Plant,** www.ianplant.com and www.shuttermonkeys.com: "I spend about 80% to 90% of my time working on my business.

"My best business advice: I always tell aspiring photographers to focus on their business, not their photography. Don't worry about chasing the latest social media photo fad or trying to take photos that will appeal to the internet masses. Instead, take the photos that you want to make.

"If you have a solid business and marketing strategy, you will find the audience that appreciates your work, and more important, you will find the customers that want to purchase your goods and services.

"But the business model needs to be your single greatest priority whenever you aren't taking photos. I've seen great photographers languish in obscurity, and bad photographers make lots of money. What sets them apart is having a good business plan and marketing strategy.

"The single smartest thing you can do to make money is to aggressively grow your email marketing mailing list. It's really difficult to engineer a hugely successful social media presence, and even then, you aren't necessarily connecting with potential customers. Figure out who your target customers are, and then find ways to get in front of them and acquire email addresses.

"I spend a huge amount of time doing presentations with camera clubs and conferences, and each time I do so, I figure out the best way to acquire email addresses from participants.

"Over time, your list can grow to have thousands, or even tens of thousands, of email addresses, and this direct marketing list allows you to directly communicate with your biggest fans, followers, and customers, without having to cut through all of the social media noise."

Sean Bagshaw, www.outdoorexposure.com: "I spend about 80% of my time on my business.

"My best business advice: 1) Immerse yourself in the thing you are passionate about long enough and you will eventually become sought out as an 'expert' in that field. 2) Never take business advice from Sean Bagshaw."

Lewis Kemper, www.lewiskemper.com: "I spend about 70% of my time focusing on my business.

"My best business advice: Nurture all business relationships. Meet as many people in the photo industry as you can and keep in touch with them. Put yourself out in front of as many people as you can."

Scott Bourne, www.scottbourne.com: "I spend 80% of my time selling/marketing and 20% creating images/video.

"My best business advice: Start every conversation about price with the following question: 'What's your budget?' This lets you know if this is the kind of client you want and also gives you an idea of how much you can safely charge. If the person you are negotiating with has a lot of experience, assume that he/she offered a budget number that is lower than the real number."

Richard Bernabe, www.richardbernabe.com: "Pre-pandemic, I spent about 70% of my time on my business and about 30% taking pictures. Post–March 2020, it was 95% on my business and only about 5% making photographs.

"Focus on your business is my best business advice."

My best business tip, one that can help you with many aspects of your business—including interacting on social media, giving seminars and webinars, recording online classes and podcasts, and writing a book or magazine article—is to take the Dale Carnegie (www.dalecarnegie.com) course, "Effective Communication and Human Relations." If you can't take the course live or online (it's not cheap), I suggest reading the Dale Carnegie & Associates book, *How to Win Friends and Influence People in the Digital Age.*

Both Susan and I took the course in the mid-1980s. We both say: "Taking the course was the best business decision we ever made." We learned how to give effective presentations and how to improve our communication skills, which includes a very important aspect of having a conversation: listening.

About listening: as photographers and presenters, we all need to listen to the audience when posting on social media, and when giving seminars and webinars. When we record an online class or write a book or blog post, we need to "listen" in advance to any questions the viewer or reader may have.

Take a listen to a few of my favorite quotes on listening:

> *"When people talk, listen completely.*
> *Most people never listen."*
> —Ernest Hemingway

*"We have two ears and one tongue so that we*
*would listen more and talk less."*
—DIOGENES

*"Most of the successful people I've known are the ones who do*
*more listening than talking."*
—BERNARD BARUCH

While you are awake, it's important to build your brand because it's what draws people to your website and social media real estate, and because it's what makes people trust you, and, in the case of making money while you are sleeping (and awake), buy from you.

Basically, your brand is you (to the public, not to your family and close friends). As Jeff Bezos, founder of Amazon, said, "Your brand is what other people say about you when you are not in the room." Here's another way to look at your brand: It's your reputation.

*Before* telling the world about your brand, you need to *build* your brand. The key, I feel, is to be yourself, and to let your personality and passions shine through. Those attributes should be summed up in your mission statement or tag line.

My friend Art Wolfe's mission statement sums up what he feels people will get from his books, workshops, and seminars: "Explore. Create. Inspire." With these three words you get a good idea of why you want to hang out—in person or on the pages of one of his many books— with Art.

When I worked in the advertising industry we had meetings during which we discussed strategies, objectives, and tactics. In developing your brand, *strategize* about the ways in which you can spread the word (social media, for example), fulfill your *objectives* (filling workshops, selling books and prints, etc.), and hone your *tactics* (a daily practice for your business).

Another important step in building your brand is having a logo. If your brand takes off, you will not even need to use your name when publishing a print on social media. The Nike Swoosh (a check mark shape) and the CBS eye are two good examples of effective logos.

You can have a logo designed by an online logo designer. I had mine designed by Hudson Valley Graphic Design here in Croton-on-Hudson, New York. The process of creating a logo requires a lot of reflective thinking, which is a good thing!

Signatures can also become your logo. For a unique signature logo, check out www.fontbros.com. You can design a unique signature/logo there.

Well, my friend, if you know your audience and build your brand, you will be on your way to running a successful business and making a few bucks, which will allow you to do what you love most: take pictures.

After you've built your brand, it's time to promote that brand everywhere possible on the web. You need to be your own PR (public relations) person because no one will work harder for you than you will.

Put the time in while you are awake—tweet, post on Instagram, Facebook, and other social media sites, etc.—and folks will come to you in the middle of the night to see what you are doing, which includes selling stuff.

I'll talk more about social media in **Chapter 3: Socialize or Succumb.** For now, it's important to keep in mind that social media is the key, not only to building your brand but, to building your audience . . .

which, in turn, is the key to making money while you are asleep as well as when you are awake.

My friend and fellow KelbyOne instructor, Tim Wallace (www.ambientlife.co.uk), has done an excellent job of building his brand, and I think we can all learn a lot from this talented photographer.

Following is an extract from an interview Tim did with Eric Minton, a Washington, D.C., writer for an article entitled, "Ninety Percent of Your Business Is How You Conduct Yourself." I learned about this interview from one of Tim's posts in the Photo Therapy Facebook Group.

In the interview, Tim shares his "Top Ten Business Tips." I agree with nine of Tim's recommendations. But when it comes to #4, I feel that not specializing can be a good thing. In fact, when I am asked, "Rick, what's your specialty?" I say, "My specialty is not specializing."

Hey, my philosophy works for me, and Tim's works for him. As my dad used to say, "To each his own."

Here are Tim's top-10 business tips:

1. People say you only live once. That isn't true. You only die once. You live every day so make every single day count.

2. Definition of 'tomorrow': a mystical land where 99% of all human productivity, motivation, and achievement are stored. Most businesses don't grasp 'today.'

3. To get good at something, it takes 10,000 times of doing it to become unconsciously competent, so get on with it.

4. People say, 'If I shoot everything, I'll get more work.' That's a mistake. You need to specialize from the very start.

5. Your brand is you and what you shoot. Your professionalism

is your business card. How you make your clients feel is your trademark.

6.  If you don't have a clear vision of what you're going to do, what you're going to shoot, and how you're going to shoot it, then you don't know what your market is. If you don't know what your market is, you don't know who your clients are. If you don't know who your clients are, you're shooting in the dark.

7.  One of the hardest things: When you start a business, you don't anticipate the fact that you lie, and the one person you lie to most is yourself. You've got to get that under control and be honest with yourself. If you really want to achieve something you will find a way, if you don't then you will always find an excuse....

8.  If you're losing customers based on price, you're on the freeway with everybody else doing the same thing in a whirlpool charging less and less. That's not going to end well. If your customer is going to base purely on price, that's the wrong customer. Don't be a cost, be an asset....

9.  You will never experience success and never truly understand success until you've been through failure. Failure is education. It shows you not just how to do something, it shows you what doesn't work. Plan to succeed but expect to fail. I've built failure into my business schedule because it will happen so prepare for it so you can overcome it and grow as well as learn.

10. Don't try to be the next me. Be the first you.

It's true, Tim is an excellent businessperson—a skill that complements his photography expertise. Spend some time on his website to see the work of someone who is a master of his craft—and someone who is a good example of specializing. 😊

I started this chapter with three quotes, so I thought I'd end with three quotes specific to making money. I think they are self-explanatory.

*"I'd like to live as a poor man with lots of money."*
—PABLO PICASSO

*"Invest in as much of yourself as you can,*
*you are your own biggest asset by far."*
—WARREN BUFFETT

*"There is only one boss. The customer. And he can fire*
*everybody in the company from the chairman on down,*
*simply by spending his money somewhere else."*
—SAM WALTON

# 2.

# YOUR WEBSITE:
# YOUR 24/7 STORE

*"Your customers don't care about how much you know,*
*until they know how much you care."*
—DAMON RICHARDS

As I mentioned earlier in this book, I know you want the world to know that you are a good photographer. You may even want to save the world, or at least a species or habitat, with your photography. Or, through your photography, you may want to bring a greater awareness to a cause.

I get it. You are not alone. Never give up your hopes and dreams. However, to achieve your hopes and dreams, you need to be a good businessperson—unless you are über talented and get discovered overnight.

All of my successful pro photographer friends are good businesspeople. Some are excellent businesspeople.

As a businessperson, you have a golden opportunity to generate income while you are awake and while you are asleep. The opportunity is your store—your website—which is open twenty-four hours a day, seven days a week. What's more, it's open to customers worldwide.

Before I share some tips for generating income from your website (which I'll call your store for the rest of this chapter), don't overlook the "open to customers worldwide" element. When creating content, think about your potential audience, not just local, regional, and national viewers, think about worldwide viewers as well.

Here are some tips for generating income even when you are not "in" your store.

**Think Like a Delicatessen Owner.** My guess is that there are several delicatessens in your area. I also guess that you have a favorite—the one you go back to again and again.

Two more guesses: you prefer the food, staff, and feeling of the store over the other delis that may be closer or more convenient.

Apply these qualities to your store:

- You need to have good content, because on the web, content is king. Always keep that in mind.
- You need to be friendly. You need to treat everyone who comes into your store as if they were coming into a local deli, or bakery, or coffeehouse, etc. "You never know who is watching," as my mother used to say. The person who clicks on your Contact button on your website and sends you an email could be a millionaire who wants to purchase your products or services.
- Your website needs to have a good "atmosphere" and feeling. A white background is more inviting than a black background, and an easy-to-read font is more inviting than a fancy, difficult-to-read font.
- Like a returning customer at the deli, you want folks to return to your site again and again. An interesting blog (discussed later in this chapter) will help you get return readers/customers.

**Grab Someone's Attention/Attract a Customer.** There are several ways to grab a potential customer's attention when they click on your store, but in my opinion, none beats a good and simple design that includes an image or images with impact. The opposite of that philosophy is having a store with music (because people are more particular about their music than their photography), fancy slide shows, and the worst offender, a huge © over the main photo with a tagline: $250,000 fine for copying any image without written permission. I have seen that more than a few times.

WordPress.com, Squarespace.com, and Wix.com, among others, offer easy-to-use templates that are a good starting point for websites.

As always, keep potential customers in mind. Use photographs that make the potential buyer say, "I'd like to get that product" (just like the deli owner uses photographs that say, "I'd like to get that sandwich").

**Include Affiliate Links.** In the **Introduction,** I touched on using affiliate links. I'll dive deeper into that particular passive income pool in **Chapter 4: The Advantage of Affiliate Programs.** For now, keep in mind that affiliate links are perhaps the easiest way to generate passive income.

**Have Buttons/Icons for Books, Classes, Galleries, etc.** A good deli owner takes pride in how he displays, arranges, and lays out his product. He wants to make it easy for you to find, and buy, an item. It's the same with your store. You want to make it easy to navigate. Remember, not all visitors to your store may be as web savvy as you.

Have easy-to-find buttons or icons so folks can get to your products and services quickly and easily.

**Blog on a Regular Basis.** Post often on your blog. The more you post, the more folks will have a reason to return to your site. And be sure to add affiliate links so you can make a few bucks for putting in the effort.

Also, posting "new on my blog" on social media is a way to get folks to visit your store.

As my friend Skip Cohen, president of Skip Cohen University (www.skipcohenuniversity.com), points out: Your website is about what you sell, but your blog is about what's in your heart. They work together like advertising and publicity, each giving the other credibility. So, with great content being *king*, photographers need to build their readership, which is key to brand awareness, reputation, and eventually sales.

**Set Up Galleries.** I'll talk more about this in **Chapter 16: Sell Prints Online,** but for now, selling your photos through e-commerce sites, such as SmugMug.com, can be profitable, and much less work than printing and shipping photographs yourself. Here, as with the other elements of your website, think international, not just local.

**Give Stuff (Educational Stuff) Away for Free.** Your free stuff can be an eBook or an online class. On my Recent Books page on my website, I give away an eBook called *Life Lessons We Can Learn from Mother Nature.*

Part One is filled with quotes that apply to the pictures. For example, I have a picture of three polar bears walking on ice, and the quote reads: Every mile is two in winter. Part II features the same photographs accompanied by technical data and a photo tip for each photo. For my polar bears shots, I share this tip:

> Camera exposure meters can be fooled by scenes with lots of bright areas—snow and sand for example. As a starting point for a good exposure, set your camera's exposure compensation feature to +1.

In the book I have "ads" for two of my other books, *Photo Therapy* and *Photo Pursuit.*

I promote *Life Lessons We Can Learn from Mother Nature*—and the fact that it's free—on social media. That results in folks coming to the book page on my website because everyone likes something for free. That book is listed at the bottom of the page, so visitors to that page see that I have several other recent books.

The bottom line—literally the bottom line of this technique—is that folks who look for and/or get *Life Lessons* purchase other books throughout the day when I am awake or taking my daily nap.

**Be Current.** In your posts, be timely. Follow trends in the photography industry (or travel industry if that is your field). Become an expert.

**Tell Stories.** Rather than just sharing facts, weave them into a story. For example, when I'm talking about my experiences on a foot safari in Africa, I could choose to only share the facts: "I was on a foot safari in Africa, I was tired as heck, and the camp was not that close." Or, I could say: "We had been out since dawn on a foot safari, which is an incredible way to observe wildlife. It was getting late in the day when, because I was exhausted, I asked my guide, 'How far is it back to camp?' He replied, 'Well, it's not that far, but it's not that close.'"

Stories, plus a bit of humor, are often more interesting to read than facts.

**Think About Your Audience.** Think about your audience not only as customers, but also as a family. I have done this in my workshops and on photo tours, and I can tell you that it works. Many repeat clients are more like family than customers, and some have even stayed at my house.

**Check Your Stats.** Most website hosting companies let you check your stats. SquareSpace, the web hosting company I use, calls this Analytics. I can check the number of page views, I can check when folks clicked on a page, the source, including my social media sites, Google, Facebook, other websites, and so on.

*Figure 1 - Checking Analytics helps you see what you are doing right, and wrong.*

I check the stats often to see how my site/store is doing. If a page needs more traffic, it's time for me to encourage, via social media, folks to come into or back to my store.

Entire books and blog posts have been written on how to design a website. Here's me summing up thousands of words: keep it simple, inviting, and attractive. And when it comes to passive income, make ordering super-easy.

Good luck with your store. I hope it's a big success.

# 3.
# SOCIALIZE OR SUCCUMB

*"Social networks aren't about websites.*
*They're about experiences."*
—MIKE DiLORENZO

In the previous chapter I outlined some important ideas for running your website, your 24/7, open-around-the-world store. If you haven't read that chapter, I'd suggest taking a look before you read about social media because many of the same practices that apply to your website apply to social media posts.

And yes, this is another thing you need to do before you doze off.

If you consider your website your store, one of the main goals of social media is to send folks to your store, have them stay there a while, hopefully learn something, and then eventually buy something. You also want visitors to return to your store and to recommend your store to others.

Social media is the key method for achieving that goal. Yes, it's free, or should I say, it can be free. "Free" posts on social media don't reach your entire following, or even a large part of your following for that matter. For greater reach, you'll need to buy ads. I'll talk about ads at the end of this chapter. I put ad talk at the end of the chapter because although it's good to know about ads and you may want to try using them, I and most of my friends don't use them to promote our products and services.

To begin, let's take a look at how you can maximize your efforts on social media. However, before we do that, I'd like to explain the title for this chapter, **Socialize or Succumb.**

When I started out in the photography industry, the phrase was "publish or perish," which applies to many art forms, especially writing. Basically, the idea was that you had to tell people what you were doing, otherwise you might perish (go out of business).

Today, I have translated that saying to "socialize or succumb." In other words, it means that you must use social media, as well as mailing lists, to tell the world what you are doing or else you will succumb (go out of business).

**Listen.** When thinking about the important aspects of social media, I am reminded of my days at Berklee College of Music, where I majored in arranging and composition. One of my classes was on ear training. Not only did we learn to hear different notes, in my opinion we also learned something even more important: how to listen.

For musicians who play with other musicians, listening is essential in order to play as a group. If you don't listen, you may play too loud, too soft, too fast, too slow, and so on.

When thinking about the important aspects of social media, I am also reminded of something that I learned while taking that Dale Carnegie course: when having a conservation, listening is more important than talking.

So, after you post, check back from time to time to listen to what folks are saying. If they like what you said, they may retweet or share your post. If they take the time to make a comment, take the time to comment on their comment. This interaction is what social media is all about—being part of a community and sharing.

Also, don't use social media exclusively to promote your stuff. I suggest using a ratio of 1:4—one promotional post for every four educational, informative, and fun posts.

**Use Eye-Catching Images.** For photographers, social media is about photography. Pick an image that has impact— one that will arrest people's scrolling habit. Consider how the image may look cropped when you post it. If the crop ruins the photo, use another photo. Also consider (and test) how an image will look on different devices.

**Create Attention-Getting Text.** Get to the point fast. Make it interesting, fun, and informative. Give a call to action.

Use a custom Bitly.com link that relates to your product. For example, if you are selling a book on the rainforest, at the back end of the link, use something like, rainforestbook4U. These custom Bitly links not only save character space, but they make your post more interesting and emphasize your product.

**Tag Friends.** Tagging friends is important. If they like what you say, they may forward your post. Here, too, don't overdo it. Don't wear out your welcome.

**Add Hashtags.** Hashtags help people join a larger conversation. They can help you build your audience. You want to use one to three hashtags per post. More than that and your post gets "muddy."

**Tag Companies and Add Company Hashtags.** Tagging companies and adding a hashtag for a company can help your post get shared by that company, as well as by your followers who use the products and services offered by that company. For example, when I share an image taken with a Canon camera and lens, and mention Canon in a Tweet or Facebook post, Canon often likes and retweets/shares that post on their own social media pages. Canon's social media pages have several million followers.

Better yet, Canon, one of my sponsors, posts my photos with my links on their social media platforms several times a year. Since Canon has millions of followers, as opposed to my thousands of followers, that's the best deal in town.

If you have a sponsor, which I talk about in **Chapter 13: Strive for Sponsorship**, your sponsor will be happy that you are spreading the word about their products or services, which may help you keep your sponsorship. If you don't have a sponsor and mention a particular product, you may have a chance at sponsorship.

**Network**. Social media is great for networking. It can help you make new friends and business associates. Here's one example: I followed pro photographer Richard Bernabe for many years. I saw his posts on Twitter and started to retweet his posts and make comments. He started to do the same.

After a few months, we were sending each other direct messages. Then we started to email each other. It turned out that we shared a mutual respect for each other.

We became friends, even though we'd never met. We still haven't had our first IRL (In Real Life) get together. The pandemic has cost us all so many good things. Yet, we became such good friends that Richard took the time, a lot of time, to write the foreword to my book, *Photo Quest: Discovering Your Photographic and Artistic Voice*. I can't tell you how much that means to me.

Today, I retweet Richard's posts about his books and workshops. I am happy to do so because I feel, and I know Richard feels, that we are all in this together.

So, if you have that we-are-all-in-this-together attitude, you will make friends. And in the photo industry, having friends is a good thing.

**Analyze This.** Social media sites let you check analytics, including the number of impressions, total engagements, media engagements, link clocks, times people read your post, and number of shares (retweets, for example, on Twitter).

These analytics can help you craft a social media strategy, that way you maximize time spent at social media marketing.

**Buy Ads.** As I mentioned at the beginning of this chapter, you'll need to buy ads on social media to increase your reach. Do they work? Well, it depends. It depends on whether or not folks want what you are promoting, and it depends on whether or not they can afford it. So, knowing your audience is key.

I know a photo workshop manager who said that they get most of their clients from Facebook ads. The company spends a few hundred bucks a month to promote their photo workshops, which cost several thousand dollars.

Personally, I have seen little result from spending money on these ads. The reason may be that folks already have my books or follow me on all my social media channels and my website. My advice would be to give it a try without breaking the bank.

Here's a brief look at what ads may cost on Twitter and Facebook and the potential audience reach in 2021.

**Twitter:** On Twitter, you create an ad by clicking on the Analytics icon below your tweet, then clicking on Promote Your Tweet. You first choose the Location, Age Range, and Gender. Then you choose your Budget, which can cost you a little or a lot.

For example, on my Twitter account, a daily budget of $50 over seven days (or $350) would net an estimated reach between 1.5K and 3.6K per day. A daily budget of $100 per day for seven days would net an estimated reach between 2.9K and 7.3K per day.

The rates and reach go up: if I spent $5,000 a day for 30 days, I'd be investing $150,000 on Twitter ads.

Keeping all this in mind, I, and virtually all of my photographer friends and associates, have never spent money on Twitter ads, but some of my friends who own photo companies have.

**Facebook**: On Facebook, you create an ad on your business page by clicking on Boost Post. Like Twitter, you can choose your audience and budget, but you can also choose People Who Like Your Page, People Who Like Your Page and Friends, people in your area, and specific interests, like birds or guitars.

On my page, a five-day ad for $50 would reach between 1.5K and 4.4K people. A 10-day ad for $100 would reach the same number of people, but for twice as long. You also have the option of having your ad appear on Instagram.

If you have never tried an ad on social media, go for it a few times. You'll learn soon enough if an ad is working or not.

Need some tips on posting on social media? Check out my friend Trey Ratcliff's book (available on Amazon.com), *Under the Influence: How to Fake Your Way into Getting Rich on Instagram: Influencer Fraud, Selfies, Anxiety, Ego & Mass Delusional Behavior*. I don't agree with everything Trey recommends, but the book really is a good read.

Here are two personal stories that illustrate the power of social media.

**One:** It was the day before Father's Day 2021. I checked sales (which authors can access 24/7) of my three Amazon self-published books and noticed that there weren't any sales. I hopped on Twitter and shared a photo of a book cover and a Tweet: "It's not too late to get your dad, or a friend who's a dad, a Father's Day gift. On Amazon, it's easy to gift a Kindle book (readable on any device). See my latest books here: ricksammon.com/ricks-books."

Before I went to sleep, I checked my sales again. Seven paperback books were sold. As I mentioned in the introduction of this book, the royalty on a $10 paperback book is about $7. So, from the three minutes it took me to compose and post a Tweet, I made $49 (assuming only that Tweet generated sales).

Sure, $49 is only a bag of peanuts, but I can trade that bag for a pizza dinner for two, compete with a nice salad and a bottle of chianti with Susan.

**Two:** From time to time, my book, *Photo Therapy*, hits #1 on Amazon in different categories. When that happens, I take a screen grab of the book and its rating on Amazon and post it on all my social media channels. That's right! More sales, more peanuts, more pizza.

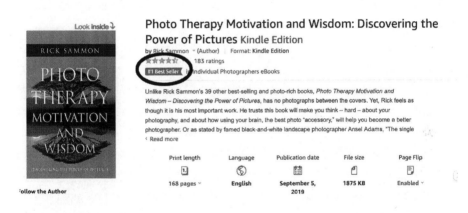

*Figure 2 - Share the good news when your book is #1 Best Seller on Amazon.*

# 4.

# THE ADVANTAGE OF
# AFFILIATE PROGRAMS

*"Making money is art and working is art,*
*and good business is the best art."*
—ANDY WARHOL

As I mentioned in the **Dedication** of this book, my dad gave me some valuable advice when I was growing up: "It takes a lot of peanuts to feed an elephant." In other words, he was saying that all those pennies can add up. Affiliate programs, also known as Associate Programs, are a good way to generate pennies and even a few dollars.

To recap what I mentioned in the **Introduction** for this book, an affiliate or associate program is a system that lets you earn a very small percentage of a sale by posting a custom-for-you, company-generated link to a product. The more links you post—on your website, on social media, and in your newsletters—the more peanuts you make.

Let's take a look at how a few affiliate programs work, starting with one of the biggest: Amazon. Keep in mind that the following information applied to Amazon's Associate Program in 2021.

**Amazon Associate Program.** One of the interesting things about Amazon's program is that the percentage you get for a referred sale varies from product to product. For example, Amazon pays you 10% for luxury beauty products, 6% for musical instruments, 4% for shoes, and 2% for television sets.

Here's a cool feature of the Amazon affiliate program: after someone clicks on your specific link, you get some peanuts for all the stuff they buy for twenty-four hours. What's more, if they put an item in their cart and don't buy it for up to eighty-nine days, you still get the payment.

As a member of the program, you can check on what folks are buying via your link. (Amazon does not share personal information about the buyer, so you see the item, but not the person's name.)

The biggest item someone bought from one of my links was a huge flat-screen TV.

*Figure 3 - After clicking on your Amazon product link, you get a small commission for all the stuff the customer buys generated from that link for 24 hours.*

The smallest item someone bought was (no kidding) a Christmas rubber ducky assortment, so my payment was very small. Other items I have seen in my reports include makeup, car radiator hoses, and tennis shoes—all unrelated to photography.

To find out more about how you can become an Amazon Associate, which is relatively easy, just type "Amazon Associate" into Google.

Before you start filling out the form, check to make sure that the program is legal in your state. At the time of this writing, you can't utilize the program if you live in the following states: Arkansas, Colorado, Missouri, Maine, Rhode Island, and Vermont. The reason has to do with taxes.

**Adorama and B&H Photo/Video.** Adorama and B&H Photo are two of the largest camera stores on the planet. Each offers an affiliate program that is easy and free to join.

Adorama offers a 2% base commission with performance-based incentives.

B&H Photo/Video also offers a 2% base commission on most products, and an 8% commission on select products.

Now, I know those percentages may not sound like a lot of peanuts, but all those peanuts can add up. For example, say you are a pro who specializes in bird photography and who runs workshops. Photographers who come on your workshops or who visit your site may buy a $2,000 lens. Your 2% commission: $40. If two people buy a $2,000 lens, you have generated enough to take your spouse or friend out to dinner.

I chose a bird photographer as an example because I know a famous bird photographer who generates enough income from a camera store affiliate program (part of his site looks like a store) that he can go out to eat almost every night of the week (maybe not to a fancy restaurant, but he can have a nice meal at a local pizza place).

Perhaps one of the most successful photo affiliate program participants is Ken Rockwell (www.kenrockwell.com). Check out his site to see how he expertly manages his affiliate programs.

**Plug-In Companies**. The Nik Collection by DXO and ON1 software are two other companies that offer affiliate programs. As an affiliate, you also get a discount code, maybe 10% or 15%, that you can pass along to your followers—so you all win.

**Software and Online Training Companies**. Adobe.com offers an affiliate program, as does KelbyOne.com. Check out their sites to see how the programs work.

**Manufacturers**. Some manufactures offer direct affiliate programs, which have a higher percentage rate than if the same product is sold by a major camera store, like Adorama or B&H. Westcott (www.fjwestcott) and Breakthrough Photography (www.breakthroughphotography.com) are two examples.

When you are on a company's website, poke around to see if they offer an affiliate program.

**Photographers**. Some photographers offer affiliate programs. Joel Grimes (www.joelgrimes.com) is one example. Joel sells many online training courses. If you send someone to Joel's site for an online class and they buy the class, you get a small commission.

The list of affiliate opportunities goes on and on ... and on. Put in the time to set up affiliate accounts and you will generate some peanuts, which, if they add up, can feed an elephant.

# 5.

## BUY ME A COFFEE

*"It's amazing how the world begins to change*
*through the eyes of a cup of coffee."*
—DONNA A. FAVORS

My friend Scott Bourne and I have a lot in common: we both love photography and we both love playing bass guitar. One thing we don't have in common: I enjoy a cup of coffee, while Scott is not a coffee drinker.

That said, Scott does appreciate it when someone buys him a coffee, but not in the traditional sense of the phrase. Rather, Scott, like some of my friends, uses the online self-funding service Buy Me a Coffee (www.buymeacoffee.com), or BMC for short.

On the "easy scale" of 1 to 5 (5 being the easiest) of how to generate passive income, Buy Me a Coffee comes pretty close to getting a 5-star rating.

Speaking of coffee, I'm taking a short break from writing this book to grab a cup, so I'll let Scott explain how he uses the service. Grab a cup and take a listen!

 Buy me a coffee

a Supporter
is worth
a 1000
followers.

*Figure 4 - Buy Me a Coffee is a cool way to generate a few extra bucks,*
*perhaps for coffee and snacks with a few friends.*

**Scott Bourne**—I recently started using Buy Me a Coffee to see if I could get away from providing ad-supported content, and yet still earn a little money for all the online teaching and sharing I do about photography.

It's a free site to use. You can create content directly on BMC and then share it with your existing (or future) audience. If you already use WordPress or Medium for your website, etc., you can put a button on your existing site linking to BMC.

BMC works sort of like Patreon.com. You provide content and your followers can send you money in return. You can sell "extras," such as workshops or eBooks. These extras also can be offered for free. This is the more transactional side of BMC. In addition, you can just publish posts (think blog posts) and then BMC adds a donate button. If people like your work, they can buy you a virtual "coffee." *Note:* You can make your "coffee" anything you want. In my case, it's Diet Coke, because as Rick knows, I am not a coffee drinker.

To be successful on BMC, you need to fully build out your profile. The more information you provide here, the better. You will also need to regularly update the site with new content. You can post anything from gear reviews to full-on how-to tutorials. Right now (mid-2021), you cannot use the site to podcast, but BMC says that feature is coming soon.

While I am not money motivated, those of you who are can build out memberships and goals. This will help you get contributions more quickly.

You can use Stripe or PayPal as your payment processor. I use PayPal. For every $3 virtual Diet Coke I sell, I get $2.46. PayPal takes a cut and so does BMC. It seems like a very reasonable cut to me, so I don't even think about it.

Summing up, I have received donations on BMC. I won't be buying any Corvettes with the money I make there, but it is free to set up, charges only a 5% transaction fee, and offers up a way to get compensated for my efforts without bombarding people with advertisements. I feel like it has been more than worthwhile.

I don't see a downside to trying BMC. If you have content to share and want to start "collecting peanuts," go for it.

To better understand how I actually use BMC, visit my BMC profile: www.buymeacoffe.com/scottburne.

**P.S.** There is another service called Ko-Fi (www.ko-fi.com) that does something similar but costs $6 a month to use. I have not tried it, but it may be worth your while to investigate.

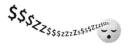

**Rick here:** I have my own P.S. to add to this chapter. Back in 2009, it was Scott Bourne who *told* me, not suggested to me, that I must be on Twitter. I was hesitant but I acquiesced. It was excellent business advice.

Scott also invited me to co-host his popular Photofocus podcast. That was fun, and it was also good for my business.

Scott Bourne is one of the best photo businesspeople I know. He continues to use new online tools, like BMC, to reach new people and to stay in touch with his fans.

If you are looking for a talented photographer to follow, follow Scott Bourne. He is also one of the most amazing bird photographers I know.

Next time I see Scott, the Diet Coke is on me!

# 6.

# START A FACEBOOK GROUP

*"The need for connection and community is primal, as fundamental as the need for air, water, and food."*
—DEAN ORNISH

Starting a Facebook group is super easy—*and free!* If you do a search on how to start and manage one, you'll learn how you can be up and running in a matter of minutes.

At the time of this writing, there are about 400 million Facebook groups. I started *Photo Therapy* in March 2020, during the early stages of the COVID-19 pandemic. It was an unplanned follow-up to my book, *Photo Therapy Motivation and Wisdom—Discovering the Power of Pictures*, published the previous year.

At the time of this writing, we have more than five thousand members from all over the world. That number, and how fast membership grew, actually surprises me, as I did not think photographers really needed another place to "hang out" online.

I feel as though the techniques I used for building *Photo Therapy* can help you start and manage a Facebook group. Although it may not be your main goal (and was not and is not mine), a Facebook Group can generate income in several different ways. I'll discuss monetizing later in this chapter.

While you're reading about my techniques and practices, keep in mind that today I still follow many of them while I maintain *Photo Therapy*, which is good fun and good photo therapy for all—including me.

One of the reasons for the group's popularity, I think, was timing. During the pandemic photographers needed an escape from reality, a safe place to share photographs, and to learn from others.

*The ever-all-important* networking (which I talk about in the **Acknowledgements & Networking** section of this book) is another reason for its success. I invited my social media followers to join the group, and I asked my photographer friends to post news about the group on social media.

As we grew, I asked a few trusted friends to be moderators, and they invited their friends. More networking.

In the early days, we held photo review Zoom sessions that we called, "Photo Therapy Happy Hour." During those free sessions members could learn photo and Photoshop techniques and have fun.

Some of the Photo Therapy Happy Hour sessions featured guest interviews. We interviewed guests, including "The Big Cat People," Jonathan and Angela Scott, both of whom have contributed to this book.

After being Zoom bombed twice (which was very embarrassing) we dumped Zoom and started a *Photo Therapy* YouTube channel where we posted the live sessions. Every time a new session was posted I promoted the session on all my social media channels, and this, of course, resulted in more members.

About a year after I started the group, I invited my dear friend, Linda Marshall, who teaches meditation, to host Monday Meditations live on our YouTube channel. These sessions were another member benefit, and a benefit for Linda in that it helped her build her audience.

Around the same time Linda and one of our mutual friends, Alec Arons, started a coaching series called, "Sharpen Your Focus." I gladly invited Linda and Alec to promote their sessions on Photo Therapy. More networking and another benefit for our members.

Last but not least, I spent, and still spend, about an hour or more a day liking and commenting on members' photographs. A few times a week I take a screen shot of a member's photograph, enhance it in Photoshop or Lightroom, and post it with a suggestion. This extra investment in time is appreciated by the photographer and our members, who are constantly inviting other photographers to join the group.

Each week I also post a "Welcome" announcement to new members. Most say thank you and many existing members welcome the new members.

Our members know that the founder of *Photo Therapy* cares, a real-life example of this quote by Damon Richards: "Your customers don't care about how much you know, until they know how much you care."

My point in sharing my active involvement on *Photo Therapy* is this: as with all groups, members will look to the founder for guidance, participation, and feedback. So, if you start a group, plan on being there for your members. Scott Kelby, founder of KelbyOne, knows this quite well. He is an excellent example of how to build an online community.

The *Photo Therapy* Facebook group is yet another example of the "snowball effect." If you plan to start a group, bear in mind that it may start out with just a few "snowflakes," but if you have a good group, those small flakes can turn into a nice sized "snowball."

Many of the same practices you use to start a Facebook group can be applied to starting a LinkedIn Group. A LinkedIn Group is another tool you may want to consider to promote your business. Some of my friends have LinkedIn groups that they use to promote their Amazon books, post articles, promote events, build their mailing lists, and network with folks with similar interests.

In advance of launching your Facebook group, you need to have a clear goal as to the type of member you want to attract and have join. You also need to decide whether it will be Public (anyone can join) or Private (members need to be approved by a moderator). *Photo Therapy*, by the way, is Private.

You also need to decide whether you want to monetize your Facebook group. The advantage of monetizing, of course, is that you'll generate some income; the disadvantage is that it may turn off some members and potential members. That is why I don't monetize *Photo Therapy*.

I started *Photo Therapy* as a safe place for photographers to post pictures and get honest, and kind, feedback and as a place where there is no politics. Making the members happy and building a community is more important to me than generating income from the group.

To be honest, however, *Photo Therapy* has helped me build my brand, increase my personal audience, and has helped to sell books.

The group has also helped members who have written books to lead workshops and produce online classes because I encourage them to let our members know about their products and services—as long as their products and services involve photo education and motivation.

If you do want to monetize your group, here are a few ideas:

- Charge a subscription, a new feature that is being tested at the time of this writing (2020).
- Offer additional services, such as personal portfolio reviews or online coaching.

- Sell products via direct links.
- Sell tickets to workshops, webinars, and other live events.
- Link to products using affiliate links.
- Sell group-related merch, such as a shirt or a hat.
- Accept donations via Buy Me a Cup of Coffee (covered in **Chapter 5**) or via recurring monthly donations through Patreon or PayPal. (All these donation options can also apply to your blog, website, YouTube channel, etc.)
- Eventually sell the rights to your group.

I invite you join the *Photo Therapy* Facebook Group. You will see, as well as enjoy, amazing photographs by well-known photographers and photographers you've never heard of. You'll get inspired and be motivated, you'll learn a lot, you'll get feedback on your images, you'll make new friends—all for free!

Getting back to not monetizing a group, here's a quote to keep in mind: "If you give people what they want, you will get everything you want."

# 7.

# WRITE OR NARRATE A BOOK

*"I write to discover what I know."*
—FLANNERY O'CONNOR

As a preface to this fairly long chapter, **Part I** is about traditionally printed books and books that you can read on a mobile device or desktop, and **Part II** is about audiobooks.

## PART I: PRINTED BOOKS/EBOOKS

Okay, I know what you might be thinking: "Rick said this book that I am holding is about making money while you sleep, so how can someone write a book when they are sleeping?"

Before I answer that question, I have a question for you: Have you ever written a caption (on social media or on your website) for a photograph, describing either the content of the photograph or the technique you used to create the image?

If you have done that, you have a basic framework for writing a book because that is exactly how most of my illustrated photography books (and children's books) are set up: pictures and captions—long captions. My latest Kindle-only book (readable on any device) *Photo Pursuit: Stories Behind the Photographs*, is also set up that way.

So, my friend, you can do it, even if you don't write like Ernest Hemingway or other well-known authors. Programs like Grammarly can help you fine-tune your work. And, of course, you can hire an editor or two or three, as I always do.

On the hiring an editor note, my friend Skip Cohen, president of Skip Cohen University (www.skipcohenuniversity.com), shares this experience:

> I was the keynote speaker at a publishing conference many years ago. Guy Kawasaki—American marketing specialist, author, Silicon Valley venture capitalist, and one of the Apple employees originally responsible for marketing their Macintosh computer line in 1984—was the previous day's opener. On stage, Mr. Kawasaki shared a story about his most current book. "As I handed my manuscript over to my editor, I said, I bet you've never seen a manuscript this clean! I said that because thirty-plus people had read and proofed my manuscript. Yet, while reading my book, the editor found 1,600 mistakes."

So, my advice, Skip's advice, and the message of Mr. Kawasaki's story: hire an editor, or two.

As an addition to the idea of clean manuscripts and mistakes, in reading this book, please keep the following in mind: Aoccdring to a rscheearch pcrojet at Cmabridge Uinervtisy, it deosn't mttaer in waht odrer the ltteers in a wrod are, the olny iprmoatnt tihng is taht the frist and lsat ltteer be in the rghit pclce.

Okay, back to your question about writing a book while you are asleep: You actually can write a book in your sleep, or perhaps more accurately, get ideas for a book and find solutions to writing challenges while you are sleeping. How? Well, according to the UC San Diego News Center, psychologists from UC San Diego found that REM (rapid eye movement) sleep improves the creative process more than any other state—asleep or awake. Often the solutions to problems come to us when we are sleeping because of a phenomenon cognitive scientists call "pattern recognition."

As an aside, Paul McCartney, former member of The Beatles, says that he wrote "Yesterday" in his sleep.

But what about the actual writing? Well, that could take months or even years. So, as I mentioned in **Chapter 1: Before You Doze Off**, you do have to work while you are awake. But once your book is published, it can generate income 24/7 for years to come.

Let's talk about the **how** and **why** of writing a book. I know you have at least one in you!

Before I get going with the specific tips, consider that if you are an avid blogger, you probably already have some material that will get you started. Each blog post could be reworked into a chapter, for example. It's the same with magazine articles—rework them, perhaps with new photos, for chapters in your book. I did just that for my book, *Camera Angles*, which was a collection of the weekly columns I used to write for the Associated Press.

Also consider this: many books have been written on landscape photography, portrait photography, black-and-white photography, travel photography, and so on. And guess what? More will be written and published, either in a printed version or an eBook.

My point: There's room for more photography books and more photography authors. So, what are you waiting for?

Before I share some specific tips for writing a book, I'd like to offer you some words of encouragement: Never give up. That has been my philosophy for all my books, some of which were rejected the first time around by publishers.

Here's my favorite never-give-up-story.

I had an idea for a series of 3-D children's books. The kids would wear the glasses and the photos would "pop off" the page. I pitched the idea to National Geographic, and they turned it down saying that I was using old technology. That was in 1995.

I never give up.

Two weeks after Nat Geo rejected my book, a friend of mine pitched the idea to the Nature Company. One week later, we had a contract for a series of six, 3-D children's books. The Nature Company committed to buying 30,000 copies of each book and sent us (along with our 40-year-old 3-D cameras) to Kenya, Costa Rica, and Bonaire to take the photographs for the books.

My never-give-up story was the start of the "snowball effect" that I mentioned earlier in this book. The 3-D books were so successful that the publisher of one of my other books, *Seven Underwater Wonders of the World*, commissioned us to do a 3-D book on antique airplanes. Several months later, *3-D Wings: Fabulous Flying Machines* was published.

A year later, our book, *Our Nation's Capital in 3-D,* was published by the United States Capitol Historical Society.

I have another never-give-up story. The three books in my Photo Trilogy—*Photo Therapy, Photo Quest* and *Photo Pursuit*—were all rejected (at different times) by a very well-known photo book publisher.

I never give up.

One day after *Photo Therapy* (the first book in my Photo Trilogy) was rejected, I was scrolling around on Twitter. I read about how my friend Trey Ratcliff of Stuck in Customs (www.stuckincustom.com) fame self-published his book, *Under the Influence: How to Fake Your Way into Getting Rich on Instagram*—on Amazon.com. I emailed Trey about his book, and he put me in touch with the producer of his book, Chad Robertson of Writing Nights (www.writingnights.org). I wrote to Chad, and a week later we had a deal to produce *Photo Therapy.*

I did not have a clue about self-publishing on Amazon, so it was Writing Nights to the rescue. For each book in my Photo Trilogy series, I sent Chad a Word document and the photos, and he worked his magic.

Writing Nights produced the cover design, interior layout, and provided editing services, and got my three self-published books on Amazon in both the paperback and Kindle versions (readable on any device)—each for under $2,000 (in 2021). Who could ask for more?

Before going to press, I reviewed the eBook version of each book on the free Kindle Previewer app, which shows you how the book will look on different devices—which is very important. I reviewed the paperback version as a flipbook PDF. After a few minor changes, I gave the okay and my books were uploaded to Amazon.

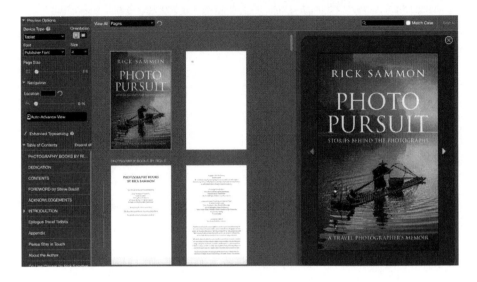

*Figure 5 - The Kindle Previewer app allows you to see how your book will look in different formats and on different devices.*

All of the books in my Photo Trilogy have been #1 best sellers (and still pop up as best sellers from time to time) and have generated some very nice passive income.

Chad also produced and uploaded this book.

I never give up, and I hope you never give up.

**FYI:** Chad Robertson at Writing Nights offers free thirty-minute consultations. If you have an idea, get in touch with Chad at: https://www.writingnights.org/p/contact-us.html.

Here are fifteen how-to tips for writing a book, tips I have followed for writing my forty-three books.

These tips apply to writing all types of how-to books, not only photography and travel books. They also apply to publishing a book with a traditional book publisher and publishing yourself on Amazon, which, again, I have found to be very profitable.

**1. Study and know your subject—inside and out.** There is an old saying: "If you want to become an expert on something, write a book about it."

Keep in mind that as well as you may think you know a subject, hire (or have the publisher hire) a technical editor or advisor. He or she will probably catch stuff you miss and mistakes you make.

**2. Know where you are going.** Before you start, have a detailed outline (which may change). If you don't know where you are going, how are you going to get there?

**3. Respect the reader.** This might be one of the most important tips. When writing each sentence, respect the reader. Remember, you are not writing the book for yourself, you are writing it for the reader. When writing your book, keep Amazon.com reviews in mind. You want as many 5-star ratings as possible, and you have a better chance of getting those ratings if you respect the reader and do your very, very best.

Speaking of reviews, disregard 1-star ratings. They are usually posted by people who have a chip on their shoulder, and who often hide behind fake names. Additionally, Amazon does not penalize an author for 1-star reviews. In fact, a review, whether a 1-star or a 5-star, counts toward "engagement"—a metric Amazon uses to determine which books to recommend and sell. A book with a hundred 5-star reviews and fifty 1-star reviews ranks much higher than a book with only a hundred 5-star reviews.

Another thing about reviews: If the reviewer is your friend or family member and sounds like they know you, as in, "I've been on Rick's workshops and he's a fun guy," Amazon may reject the review, or they may take it down.

And get this, even if one of your friends or family members tries to post a review, as in "Sammon did a good job on this book," the same thing may happen. How? Because Amazon knows who you know and does its best to prevent biased reviews.

4. **Leave no question unanswered.** Don't leave the reader asking, "Why did the author not complete that line of thought?" Go the extra mile when talking about a topic.

5. **Know your competition.** Go online and see what other authors are doing on the same subject. Ask yourself, "How can I make my book, better/different/the best?"

6. **Have more material than you think you need.** You need a lot of material to write a how-to book: photos, illustrations, and text. In planning your book, remember that one page in Word does not equal one page in your book layout

7. **Make it easy and fun for the publisher/editor to work with you.** Be flexible. I am not the best photographer or author on the planet, but I do pride myself on being perhaps one of the easiest when it comes to working together.

8. **Give your editor specific instructions.** For example, when I submit photographs, I tell my editor: "Crop my pictures and you're a dead man!" After which I add the Happy Face emoji.

9. **Plan ahead.** Never miss a deadline. Give yourself plenty of time to write … and edit, and rewrite, and rewrite, and edit, etc. Remember: Dates in your rearview mirror are closer than you think.

10. **Let your personality show/shine though.** Many other authors know what you know. What makes your book different? Your personality, your style. Write like you talk and don't try to write too fancy. Tell a few (just a few) jokes and personal stories. Let people get to know you.

11. **Have fun!** If you are not having fun writing your book, that will probably come through to your audience. Even if you are not having fun, write as though you are having fun. As I tell folks at book signings, "It's sometimes not fun writing a book, but it's always fun autographing one!"

12. **PR your book.** After your book is completed, it's really up to you

to promote the book, through social media and on your website. You are the best PR agent your book can have. Get your friends to help you promote your book, too.

**13. Set a daily word count and a final word count.** I share this tip toward the end of my list because it's somewhat optional, especially for those who don't want to put themselves under pressure. But if you are serious about getting a book published, setting word counts will help.

How much you should write a day, and how long you should spend writing, is up to you. I'd suggest giving yourself at least one hour of writing/quiet time.

The length of a book is important—the word count of this book is about 40,000, my *Photo Therapy* book is 35,000 words, and my *Photo Quest* book is 45,000 words.

As an aside, the word count of *The Great Gatsby* is 47,094 words.

**14. Ask for Feedback Along the Way.** As you develop a title, write an outline, complete a chapter, and so on, ask a loved one or trusted friend to give you honest feedback. Tell them, "Don't be afraid to hurt my feelings."

**15. Write, don't edit.** In other words, put your thoughts and ideas first, and don't be too concerned about the length of a paragraph, tense, correct grammar, punctuation, and so on. You can do that later. What's more, your editor, even if you need to hire one (I always do), can help you out with all that stuff.

The main thing is to get your ideas down first.

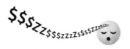

Okay! Now, let's take a look at **why** you should write a how-to book. As you will see, some of the same tips also apply for the **how** of book writing.

**1.** A paper book gives a photographer credibility, much more so than an eBook. Countless photographers have eBooks, but only a few hundred photographers have paper books (most of which are also available as eBooks). A paper book separates you from the crowd. A paper book also gives you a wonderful sense of accomplishment.

2. A paper book is *the best* calling card. For example, say you want to do a trade-off with a tourist office: some photos for a free or discounted trip. Sending a paper book is much more impressive than sending a link to an eBook. A paper book increases your chances of achieving your goal.

3. Looking for sponsors? Well, among other things, sponsors want to know if you can spread the word about their products or services. A book is a great way to prove that you can do it.

4. Speaking of doing it and proving it, writing a book is a lot of work. Having a paper book proves that you are organized and dedicated—and that a publisher believes so much in you as to invest *their* money in *your* project. When a publisher believes in you, it's easier for others to believe in you.

5. Speaking of getting organized, a book is an efficient way to organize your images, as well as your ideas. I've written forty-three books, and I "see" the chapters and pages in my head as well as on my computer, so I know where to find my pictures in the book folders on my hard drive.

6. Knowing that your images will be "set in stone" on the pages of a paper book, you just may work just a bit harder on your image editing. Once your paper book is published, there is no going back. It's the same for the words in a traditional paper book. There is no going back, so you should probably work a bit harder at the writing. FYI: One of the advantages of publishing a paper book on Amazon is that you can easily make changes.

7. Book publishers allow you to recycle some of the content of your book, usually around ten percent. So, you can transform a chapter, for example, into a paid article for a magazine, and add a promo for your book at the end of the article.

8. As I mentioned in the **how** section, book signings at seminars are fun!

9. You'll become an expert. As I said before, there's an old expression: "If you want to become an expert at something, write a book about it." It's true. While writing my books, I did a ton of research to make sure I was providing accurate information.

10. Compiling your images for a book is perhaps the best way to select your very best images from the thousands you have taken. You become your own photo editor, which is an important skill to acquire.

11. And last, but not least, you can "talk" to people when you're dead! 😃

By now you are probably asking, "What about making money?" Well, as with all things in life, it depends—it depends on the price, quality, and appeal of your book, as well your social media presence and marketing skills.

If you are working with a traditional book publisher, having a big name will help you get a big advance and a nice royalty agreement, while having a big following on social media will help sales, and vice versa.

Regarding an advance, when I published my first digital photography book in 2003, I, like most photo book authors at that time, received a $30,000 advance against royalty payments. Today, in 2021, an advance from a traditional photo book publisher might be $5,000. However, it's more likely (even for well-known photo book authors) that there is no advance. However, no advance means a higher royalty per sale for the author.

Times have changed, for sure. This is one reason why I like self-publishing on Amazon.

When it comes to publishing a book on Amazon, a big name and big social media following is the key. I discuss financial details of publishing in the **Publishing Paperback and Kindle Books on Amazon** section in the **Introduction** for this book.

Hey, you may not be able to buy a top-of-the-line BMW or Tesla with the profits from your photography book, but if it does well the profits can help out with your monthly payments for a Chevy, Ford, Honda, or Toyota.

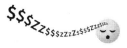

When I talk about writing a book to potential authors, I share these three quotes:

> *"There is nothing to writing. All you need to do is sit down*
> *at a typewriter and bleed."*
> —ERNEST HEMMINGWAY

> *"Writing is easy. All you have to do*
> *is cross out the wrong words."*
> —MARK TWAIN

> *"I'm writing a book. I've got the page numbers done."*
> —STEVEN WRIGHT

## PART II: AUDIOBOOKS

**Part II** of this chapter is going to be much shorter than Part I because many of the same principles for writing a book apply to audiobooks, not to mention that you actually need to write your book—your script—first.

Some photographers offer both printed/readable books and audiobooks, either on Amazon or Apple Books. Another option: self-published audiobooks.

Photographer and motivator Chase Jarvis, creator of Creative Live (an online training site), is one example. Chase's book *Creative Calling: Establish a Daily Practice, Infuse Your World with Meaning, and Succeed in Work + Life* is available in print (paperback and hard cover), eBook for Kindle, and as an audiobook.

If you like the sound of your voice, can work in a quiet area with relatively flat (no echo) sound, have time to make an articulate and virtually flawless (no coughing and "popping") recording, want to invest in a good mic and recorder (RØDE offers several excellent mics, and Zoom offers a wide range of portable recorders), go for it.

When you're "going for it," keep in mind that the recording will probably take longer, perhaps much longer, than you anticipate—mainly because you will need to do retakes, which means you will need time to edit. Unless you want to hire an audio editor, you'll need to become an editor, too.

Audio editing, however, is relatively easy. Audacity for Windows, and Garage Band and iMovie for Mac, are easy-to-use editing programs. Once you master either of these, they can make you sound like a pro. Because you can cut a clip into microseconds, editing out a mistake or a flub is a cinch.

And speaking of recording and editing, here's a very important tip: always keep editing in mind while you are recording. In other words, after a sentence or paragraph, keep in the back of your mind that you may need to go back and rerecord it. If you rush to the next word, editing may be difficult.

One final tip: before you record your entire book, do a test recording of a short chapter and send it to a few friends for their opinion; this is actually a good idea when you're writing a book, too. Listen to their feedback because, among other reasons, we hear our voices differently than others hear it.

**P.S.** You may be asking, "How come Rick does not have any audiobooks?" Well, to be honest, some folks say I have a strong New York accent and that I talk too fast. I agree, and the combination of the accent and talking fast may be a turn-off to some. Could I slow down? Sure, but then I would not sound like me.

The other reason is time: I try to exercise for forty-five minutes three times a day (two walks and a bike ride), and I like to play bass guitar for about an hour a day. Of course, I could make time to make audio recordings of my books but being healthy and having fun with my bass are more important to me at this point in my life.

# 8.

# OFFER A DOWNLOADABLE PDF EBOOK

*"Life without a Kindle is like life without a library nearby."*
—FRANZ S. MCLAREN

Offering a downloadable PDF eBook is perhaps the easiest and is definitely one of the more popular methods of generating money while you are sleeping. Assuming of course that you use a website to do all the work for you once you have uploaded your book to that site.

Let's take a look at how you can get into the self-publishing eBook market.

My guess is that you already have the makings of an illustrated PDF eBook, but you may not realize it. If you have given an in-person or online PowerPoint or Keynote presentation that can easily be transformed into a PDF (Export to PDF) with the click of mouse. It's that easy, well ... almost.

If your slide show does not have detailed information and easy-to-read text, you'll need to add that to your presentation/PDF. But it won't cost you anything to create your eBook.

I followed that technique when I was selling two of my PDF eBooks: *Life Lessons We Can Learn from Mother Nature* and *How to Get Motivated and Stay Inspired*. Each book includes fewer than a hundred images and the text is short and sweet. My tip here is to write succinctly and to try and avoid using a ton of images. One reason to avoid using a lot of images is that you want to think about the file size of your PDF and download time. You don't want folks who don't have high-speed internet to get frustrated waiting for your book. Also, I suggest thinking about a series of books where you can spread out your images throughout the series. Keep in mind that if someone buys one of your eBooks and likes it, they may buy more.

A PDF conversion from Keynote and PowerPoint is only one technique for creating an eBook, but, again, it's the easiest one. Your design, however, is much more limited compared to using, say, Apple Books or websites such as Blurb (blurb.com) and Venngage (venngage.com) that are specifically designed for creating attractive eBooks. If you want to go this route, I suggest doing a search for "how to create an eBook" and see which sites fit your needs and budget.

If you want to take your PDF to the next level, making it look and feel like an actual book, websites such as FlipBuilder (www.flipbuilder.com) and Issuhub (www.issuhub.com) let you transform your PDF into an eBook with pages that look like they are flipping as you go from page to page. This makes your book more interactive, which is a benefit for all online media.

Again, selling a PDF online is one of the easiest ways to generate passive income—if you set up a system where customers can automatically download the PDF without taking any of your waking time.

When I was selling the two aforementioned eBooks (I now give away *Life Lessons* via a Dropbox link on my site, and *How to Get Motivated and Stay Inspired* is now a KelbyOne class), I used Content Shelf (www.content-shelf.com), one of many shopping cart and e-commerce sites.

Content Shelf also offers downloadable videos, and I used them for an instructional video, *Master Landscape and Seascape Photography*, which I eventually updated for one of my KelbyOne.com live sessions.

Here's a quick look at three of their pricing packages per month (in 2021):

Premium: $14 for 25 products with 1 GB of digital storage.

Premium Plus: $29 for 100 products with 5 GB of digital storage.

Enterprise: $44 a month for unlimited products with 10 GB of digital storage.

You can also sell a PDF eBook on Amazon, but Amazon will take a small commission.

My friend Erin Babnik uses the popular e-commerce site E-junkie to sell an eBook that she worked on alongside a group of photographers called Photo Cascadia. The book, *Photographing Through the Seasons: Great Places to Photograph Each Season in the Western United States*, features two hundred and nineteen pages, one hundred photo stories, forty-nine nature tips, and sells for $19.95.

E-junkies offers a free thirty-day trial. For $20 a month, you can upload a hundred and fifty products and you get 8 GB of storage. For $40 a month, you can upload an unlimited number of products and get unlimited storage.

Speaking of pricing, pricing is key to your eBook's success. I suggest looking at other eBooks with similar content and price your book accordingly.

For some guidelines, here's a look at how my friend Denise Ippolito (www.deniseippolito.com) prices four of her more than a dozen eBooks, which she sends to customers herself, rather than using a service like Content Shelf:

*The Softer Side of Macro, Version II*: $24.

*Bird Photography: The Art of the Composition*, $24

*Impressions of Bosque del Apache II*, $16.

*Photoshop Quick Tips File III*, $10.

Denise is not only a wonderful photographer, but a savvy businessperson. Check out her work and her workshops. I promise you'll learn a lot.

One final tip. When creating a PDF eBook, before you promote it, do a test to see how it looks on different devices: smartphone, tablet, and desktop. The pages will look different on different devices, so it's not impossible that a picture that looks great on a desktop may be too small to appreciate on a smartphone.

This is one reason why I switched to Kindle books. The setup allows the book to look good on any device and allows the user to choose how the book (picture and text size) will look.

Need some ideas for a cool eBook, and want to get some for free at the same time? Go to Expert Photography (www.expertphotography.com), click the Search icon, and type in "The Big List of Free Photography Ebooks." One of my favorites here is Scott Bourne's *Nine Motivational Essays on Photography*.

Good luck with your PDF eBook. I know you have one in you!

**P.S.** Linktree (www.linktree.com), which is a website that lets you create a single link with all your important links, now lets you sell stuff, like an eBook, by adding an e-commerce link. This is a cool tool for photographers who want all their links in one, easy-to-find, place/link.

What's more, you can add a donate button for folks who want to support your creative efforts.

My Linktree page links all these sites together:

- My Website
- Learn Online with My KelbyOne Classes
- Photo Therapy Motivation and Wisdom
- Photo Therapy Facebook Group Page
- Photo Quest
- Photo Therapy YouTube Channel
- Get Motivated and Stay Inspired
- Photo Pursuit.

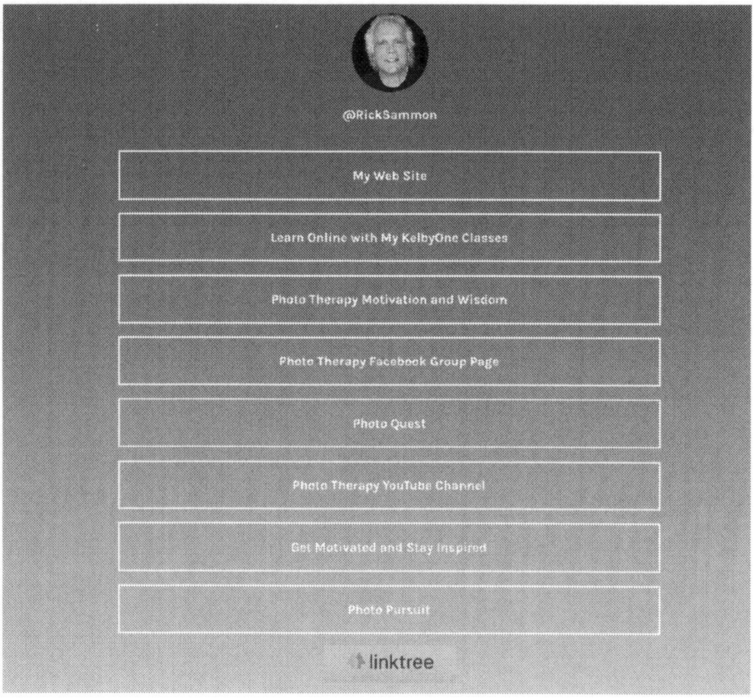

*Figure 6 - My Linktree includes links to all my important sites on the web.*

# 9.

## JOIN THE CROWD WITH CROWDFUNDING

*"Before you even start building your crowdfunding page,*
*start by building a crowd."*
—ROY MOREJON

Have you ever thought to yourself, I have a great idea for a product that I'm sure the world would love, but I just don't have the capital to get it off the ground? Plus, I'm not the type of person who wants to go on *Shark Tank* (the entrepreneurial-themed reality television show where inventors pitch their ideas to millionaires and billionaires hoping to get funding).

Well, there is a way to go, where you don't need to sell your soul or product idea to a company (I talk about pitching in **Chapter 18: Suggest a Product to a Company**) to realize your dream. The concept is called "crowdfunding."

This is the approach four of my friends—**Don Komarechka**, the mad scientist of macro photography; **Jonathan and Angela Scott**, the Big Cat People; and **Larry Tiefenbrunn**, avid photographer, and lover of photography—took to get funding for their projects.

Don's idea was to produce beautifully illustrated educational books.

Jonathan and Angela's concept was to produce a fine-art book that illustrated the wonders of wildlife, and why we should protect it and be connected to it.

Larry's idea was an original photographic invention called the Platypod, which is basically a flat camera support that can be mounted anywhere.

Their stories of success with crowdfunding are so informative that I asked them to share their experiences with you. I'm sure some readers have a unique idea for a product or may know someone who does.

While you're reading this chapter and their words of wisdom, keep one of the business philosophies that I mentioned in **Chapter 1: Before You Doze Off** in mind: You have to put in the time before you have the time.

## DON'S STORY:

One of the liberating virtues of crowdfunding is the ability to monetize a "passion project" in ways that wouldn't otherwise be possible. Publishing a book is a perfect example of this, and I have successfully created numerous crowdfunding campaigns for niche books.

If the concept of a three hundred-plus-page book on the science and photography of snowflakes was presented to a traditional book publisher, they probably wouldn't bite. It would either be flat-out rejected or stripped down to a general interest paperback.

Backed on indiegogo.com, my book *Sky Crystals: Unraveling the Mysteries of Snowflakes* was overfunded, and eventually the entire press run was sold. It was a huge financial success, and crowdfunding handled all of the expenses. Extra books were purchased, and these could be sold risk-free and on my own terms.

It wasn't all rainbows and butterflies, though. The entire first press run needed to be scrapped entirely. The press made incorrect suggestions for manufacturing process and paper types, causing the heavy amount of ink on the pages to create ripples that looked like water damage. With my reputation on the line, I had to stand up to the biggest printing company in Canada to get them to reprint the book, and I had to pay the difference in manufacturing costs.

Those lessons learned, I used the same methodology years later for my book *Macro Photography: The Universe at Our Feet*, this one funded on Kickstarter. Although this had higher production quality from a better printing facility, this book was also something that a traditional publisher probably would not have taken a gamble on. "Who cares how you photograph micrometeorites?" and, "No one will want to make their own stereoscopic 3D anaglyphs! What the heck is an anaglyph?!" I'm sure they would say.

In the end, I created a four-pound, three hundred- and eighty-four-page book with nearly ninety thousand words and hundreds of images. The book has been celebrated for being thorough and well produced, but it did not come easily.

This second project was hindered in early 2020 by the global SARS-CoV2/COVID-19 pandemic. With roughly 90% of the book completed, productivity came to a grinding halt when I was forced to switch gears to taking care of my family.

Writing a book requires focus—routinely, six hours of uninterrupted time per day to fully explore concepts and build page layouts. That time instantaneously evaporated and delayed the release of the book for a year. There were vitriolic comments from people that could not understand the delays, and it was my fault for certain gaps in communication while I focused on raising my young daughter. There's no question that there was a temporary tarnishing of my reputation in the eyes of some backers, but as the books eventually made their way into the hands of people who supported the project that reputation was restored.

There are many lessons to be learned, some of which you can only learn through personal experience. A few concepts to keep in mind generally:

- 😊 Remember that people are backing you, and your project. There's a personal connection here that can strengthen your brand over time.
- 😊 Delays are to be expected. Give yourself more time than you think you need to accomplish your goals.
- 😊 Shipping costs will always be higher than you originally anticipate!
- 😊 Find as many ways as possible to over-deliver.

I have found that putting as much of the funding into the final project as possible is the best way forward. You'll end up with extra inventory without any extra money in your pocket, with the goal to sell through that excess inventory as a long-term revenue aid. For example, say a book costs $10 to manufacture but I sell it for $75. It would make far more sense spending all the money on additional inventory, knowing that it would be sold, rather than keeping cash. I used the extra funds from my crowd-funding campaigns to buy more inventory which creates more profit if it all sells. There's a gamble with the assumption that you'll actually sell all the inventory, but it's been a successful strategy for my last two books published this way.

*Sky Crystals* took six years to completely sell through, but it was always nice to wake up in the morning knowing that another book had been sold.

Promoting the crowdfunding campaign is also full-time work during the time you have allotted for it to run. Ensure that you don't have other significant obligations during this time. My strategy was to get guest appearances on podcasts and to write articles and pitch them to various photography blogs. My efforts even resulted in radio interviews with CBC stations across Canada, and a few morning television shows.

Have an idea? Throw everything against the wall and see what sticks. You'll need your already-established audience to help you reach your funding goal, but you'll need to do everything possible to expand that audience during your campaign.

**Don Komarechka**
www.donkom.ca

## Jonathan & Angela's Story:

In February 2021, we launched our first Kickstarter campaign to fund our latest book, *Sacred Nature Volume 2: Reconnecting People to Our Planet* (HPH, September 2021). This two hundred- and eighty-eight-page fine art wildlife photography book is a companion volume to our award-winning book *Sacred Nature: Life's Eternal Dance* (HPH, 2016), which aims to reveal the wonder and beauty of our world and instill a sense of awe and concern for our world's well-being.

Across the thirty-four days of our Kickstarter campaign, we were overwhelmed by the support of so many generous backers, who helped us raise $125K to fund the book of our dreams and the Sacred Nature Initiative. The book is due to be published in September 2021. The following tips were crucial to our Kickstarter campaign's success.

**Create a Press Kit.** In preparation for our Kickstarter campaign, we wanted to ensure that we had the resources necessary to launch with plenty of buzz and press coverage. Three to four months ahead of time we began building a list of potential contacts to help promote the campaign. This included friends and family (including Rick), professional contacts, colleagues, bloggers, influencers, and fellow photographers. To that list we added relevant media outlets, including podcasts, blogs, magazines, and newspapers.

About a month before the official launch date, we created a digital press kit and distributed it to each of the contacts on the list. It contained everything necessary to successfully promote the Kickstarter campaign: press releases, image assets for digital and print media, social media captions, and image assets for various social media channels (Instagram, Facebook, Twitter, and LinkedIn).

Creating a press kit was crucial—it ensured that our promotion campaign was seamless and effective. The kindness and generosity of each and every person who helped us spread the word about the project was so gratifying.

**Offer a Variety of Rewards.** In our opinion, creating unique and compelling rewards is crucial for a successful campaign. In total, we released thirty rewards across the duration of the Kickstarter campaign—signed copies of the book, fine art prints, pen and ink drawings, and exclusive, hosted safari trips. We highly recommend spending time brainstorming creative and unique rewards that will appeal to your audience. For instance, we offered 1:1 photography critiques and virtual coffee chats for backers who wanted a more personal experience.

Once you've chosen all your rewards, release them in stages. Most Kickstarter projects experience a mid-campaign "slump," especially after the initial excitement has worn off. Having new rewards available each week keeps the project fresh and exciting. Over the course of the campaign, you will have the opportunity to see which offerings appeal most to backers and release additional quantities, as needed.

**Leverage Social Media.** Our last tip for executing a successful Kickstarter campaign is to leverage social media to amplify your messaging. This was one of the most challenging and time-consuming aspects of the campaign, but also one of the most impactful.

At every step of the campaign—whether it was announcing the launch or providing production updates—we made sure to share everything with our audience across our social channels. Certain channels, especially Instagram Stories, made it incredibly easy for us to announce the most current updates, such as when new rewards became available or when certain offers were sold out.

We used YouTube, Instagram, Twitter, LinkedIn, and Facebook to share key milestones with our audience and to consistently communicate where we were in relation to our funding goal. We also made sure to communicate with our existing backers through the "Updates" feature on Kickstarter. This was a great way to express our gratitude for their support, share project progress, and provide fulfilment instructions.

**Jonathan & Angela Scott**
www.bigcatpeople.com

## Larry's Story:

Before I was introduced to crowdfunding, my Playtpod invention started with a simple idea—a flat "tripod" that I produced on a small scale with the aid of a friend in the metal-parts manufacturing business. My wife Mina and I (yes, we are a true "mom & pop" operation) marketed the Platypod through several magazines, Facebook, and through Scott Kelby's wonderful organization, KelbyOne.

While our original product was about the size of an iPhone, we saw a lot of demand in the market for a larger unit, about the size of an iPad, so I developed the Platypod Max. But I had no idea how large my audience would be or, initially, how many to order from my manufacturer for the first production run.

It was Kickstarter to the rescue, because it essentially provides advertising to a unique crowd that likes to fund unique and innovative projects and receive a benefit/reward for doing so in return. The benefit/reward usually comes in the form of a sample of the product at a significantly discounted cost. One could think of it as a presale with some risk to the backers who have no guarantee of receiving their benefit/reward if the project fails.

I found that one of the most important elements of a Kickstarter campaign was to have a strong but brief video presentation. It was super-helpful to review some heavily funded projects, and to try to see what about their presentations really turned people on.

I found the most amazing project was something called "Potato Salad" by Zack Danger Brown where someone, as a joke, offered to make and send out samples of potato salad in exchange for crowd funding support. He ended up accumulating about $55,492 in support from over 6,911 backers!

I called some people I know and asked for their help with writing a video script. I also needed advice on hiring a videographer.

I hired a professional graphic artist to help set up a Kickstarter page which, in and of itself, has almost no significant formatting tools. Essentially, we created several long JPEG strips with the information that we wanted to impart and pasted them into the web design page on Kickstarter.

Great crowdfunding starts with a great product. That can be a book, a device, artwork, or almost anything you can imagine, but it's a good idea to poll as many people as you know and listen to their honest critiques. If you have the skills to produce a video and the artwork yourself, you can save between $10,000 and $40,000. Otherwise, be prepared to spend a good chunk of money to set up your page. Bear in mind though that if you spend too much money at the outset, you are likely to lose it.

Most Kickstarter programs are not successful. Less than 0.5% of those that do reach their goals raise over $100,000, and only about 14% produce over $20,000 in pledges. However, if you are certain you have a great idea you should go for it.

**FYI:** If your Kickstarter project is successfully funded, the following fees will be collected from your funding total: Kickstarter's 5% fee, and payment processing fees (3% plus $0.20 per pledge). Pledges under $10 have a discounted micro-pledge fee of 5% plus $0.05 per pledge. If funding isn't successful, there are no fees. (Note: These are the percentages at the time of this writing, 2021.)

At the outset, you decide a funding goal that will allow you to deliver your product. If you do not reach that goal by the end of the campaign (usually thirty to sixty days) everyone walks away with no charges, but you live to see another day. If you fail to deliver on a completed campaign, it is unlikely that you will be able to run another successful campaign on Kickstarter.

Reputation, as Rick well knows and talks about in this book, is extremely important. You must also be certain that you will be able to come through with your promise and do it reasonably on time. You will need a manufacturer you can trust to produce the product and a fulfillment center to help you deliver it around the world. There are many resources for this on the Kickstarter website.

Our first Kickstarter raised over $100,000 from one thousand, three hundred backers. The next one for the Platypod Ultra topped $225,000, and our third project for the revolutionary Platyball tripod head drew over half a million dollars from more than two thousand backers. Our fine reputation, developed in the first two projects, enabled our success on the third. The first two campaigns concluded with delivery-on-time, but the third one was delayed over eight months due to necessary mechanical redesigns and the COVID-19 pandemic.

Kickstarter requires that you give backers a monthly update. We maintained an open and honest approach and explained why we were delayed. We also endeavored to set clear expectations for ultimate delivery. Even though we were delayed, our honesty and openness should help us with other projects in the future.

By the way, I have been mentioning Kickstarter but there are other crowdfunding sites. I used Indiegogo for a follow-up program of my last campaign. It's a matter of taste as to which website you choose to host your project.

Following are some key elements for running a successful product campaign:

- Demonstrate the ability to do more with less.
- Show it as a problem solved in simple and clear language. "Here are the problems. Here's how we solved them."
- Show you looked at what was out there and didn't find it.
- The first fifteen seconds of the video must be an attention grabber, clearly demonstrating the purpose of the product from the outset. Discuss features at the end.
- Conclude the video with the big why: "Why do you need this?"
- Demonstrate that your product embodies an "elegant yet simple design."
- Get celebrity endorsements if you can. Trade shows are sometimes the best place to meet the stars in the industry.
- Last but not least, marketing is incredibly important. Make sure you have the means to put the word out on social media, such as Instagram, Facebook, and Twitter. Kickstarter itself will get the word out to its own crowd, but you should reach much further than that. Also look into companies such as Backerkit and Jellop to help you with any program that you believe will be highly successful.

If you would like to view our three Kickstarter campaigns, go to Kickstarter.com. In the search box, type in *Platypod* for the first two campaigns, or *Platyball* for our most recent one.

So, if you have the funds to get started and you can afford to take some risk and you have a great idea, then pop a few antacids and go for it!

**Larry Tiefenbrunn**
www.platypod.com

**Rick here:** In closing this chapter, I'd like to mention that while Don, Jonathan & Angela, and Larry do generate income from their projects while they are sleeping, they still work their butts off on customer support and promotion of their products while they are awake.

# INTERMISSION

*"Taking a break can lead to breakthroughs."*
—RUSSELL ERIC DOBDA

Y ou are about halfway through reading this book. In the previous and subsequent chapters, I, and some of my friends, offer suggestions about making money while you are sleeping (as well as when you are awake) and other savvy business strategies.

For now, I'd like you to take a break, and take some time to think about why you got into photography in the first place. My guess it was not to make money. Rather, you enjoyed the process of creating something original and satisfying. Simply put, it was fun.

So, take a break from focusing on the business side of photography and go out and take some pictures, or take some pictures around your house. Have fun processing those pictures. Post some pictures on social media. Ask for feedback.

Spending too much time focusing on the business side of your business can take the fun out photography.

This is especially true if you fall into the trap of checking sales and analytics (Amazon sales shown here), which can be frustrating (and addicting) when you are first starting out, and even after you have been at it for a while.

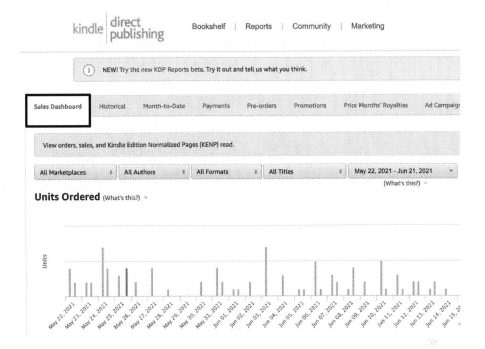

*Figure 7 - The Sales Dashboard for Kindle Direct Publishing lets you check sales 24/7.*

Maybe take a walk, which, in addition to being good for your body, is good for your mind and soul. During your walk, you may come up with some ideas. You may find this expression to be true: "Angels talk to a man who goes for a walk."

While I was writing this book (about four hours a day for three months), I took two forty-five-minute walks a day, during which I made some nice photographs. I also rode my bike for about an hour each day, took my daily power nap, and played guitar or bass for about an hour a day.

All that relaxing gave me time to think, not only about this book but about other important things in my life.

So, always remember to take a break.

Hey! If during your break you want to start reading another book, one that will inspire you to pursue your dreams and passions, I recommend *Real Magic: Creating Miracles in Everyday Life,* by Dr. Wayne Dyer. Basically, Dr. Dyer talks about how we create our own reality, which is something not everyone considers. It's my #1 self-help book recommendation. It has helped many of the photographers, and non-photographers, I know create their own reality.

Here's another idea for your break time: Start what's called a "vision board." A vision board is a board—either a physical one like a cork board that you place on a wall, or a digital one you can create on your computer—on which you place cards, notes, photos, and so on, with your visions, your ideas for future projects and goals, which may include some of the topics covered in this book. The concept is that you are reminded of your ideas on a daily basis and start to visualize those ideas.

Does visualization work? For sure, as Dr. Wayne Dyer points out in his book.

My good friend Ron Clifford (www.ronclifford.com) also agrees with the power of vision boards. Take a listen to what Ron has to say.

I made my first vision board in early 2015 and I did it rather reluctantly. After all, aren't vision boards for dreamers and in the realm of woo-woo wishful thinking? But alas, I found myself challenged to at least give it a try, and after committing to it I set out with scissors and glue and poster board and went old school on it.

On it was travel as a guide to Antarctica, do a TED talk, have a studio with old wooden floors, travel to Africa, present to audiences, and quite a few other things. Within a few days of completing the vision board, a future trip to Antarctica became a reality, and over time, everything and more listed above came true.

It turns out I was wrong (don't tell my wife I admitted that): it isn't woo-woo or wishful. It sets in place your intentions and creates a visual benchmark to give your faith something to move toward.

I am now a believer in the power of vision boards to help people have something to believe in and move toward. There is so much more to them than dreams and wishful thinking.

Thank you, Ron, for sharing your thoughts on vision boards.

Ron mentioned his wife, which reminded me of some sound business advice that I'd like to share with husbands, like myself, who work with their wives: happy wife, happy life.

And if you are a wife who works with her husband, here's some advice to share with him: happy wife, happy life!

Okay, I'll see you after intermission.

# 10.

## START A PODCAST

*"My favorite things in life don't cost any money. It's really clear that the most precious resource we all have is time."*
—STEVE JOBS

Over the past ten years, I have been the co-host of three weekly podcasts, in the following order: *Photofocus* with Scott Bourne, *The Digital Photo Experience* with Juan Pons, and most recently *Picturing Success* with Larry Becker.

I thoroughly enjoyed podcasting with Scott, Juan, and Larry. I learned a ton about podcasting, and I learned even more from the dozens and dozens of photographers I interviewed—the best of the best of top photo pros in the world. For sure, the audio-only podcasts helped me build my own brand and helped me get recognized. One example: "Hey, are you Rick Sammon?" I heard in the lobby of a hotel in Alaska. "I recognize your voice from your podcast."

We had several paying sponsors for the *Photofocus* and *Picturing Success* podcasts, and that monthly sponsorship was a nice addition to my monthly income.

So why did I bow out of all three podcasts? Time.

Yes, each podcast was only about one hour in length. But here's a look at the total amount of time it took for each show:

- 1 hour: record
- 1 hour: interview with pro
- 30 minutes: working with pro to schedule, get bio info, etc.
- 15 minutes: writing show notes, adding links, etc.
- 15 minutes: prepare for each show.
- 15 minutes: promote the show and the podcast on social media.
- 30 minutes: follow up on social media with questions.

Actual time for each show: about 3 hours and 45 minutes.

And yes, my co-hosts spent the same amount of time when they were conducting interviews for the shows, and even when they weren't, they were editing the recording, adding the ins and outs, posting on social media, posting on the show's website, promoting, and so on. Talk about time!

Again, the podcasts were fun, the income was nice, and name recognition was helpful in building my brand, but there are only so many hours in the week, and I like to do many things during those hours, including: taking and processing pictures, writing, posting on social media, riding my bike, walking, playing my guitars and keyboard, napping, and having Happy Hour with Susan.

Plus, before the COVID-19 pandemic, we took four to five trips a year, and some, like a trip to the bottom of the world, lasted two weeks or more. All that travelling required recording podcasts—sometimes three—in advance.

Summing up: I wanted more time to explore new photography projects and more time for learning new songs on my bass guitar.

I share all this with you so you can think about an important element when it comes to podcasting: time. You must have/make the time to post shows on a consistent basis. If you don't, you will lose some of your audience. And when it comes to podcasting, it's all about the audience.

It's also about reviews. Each time you prepare for, and record, a podcast keep reviews in mind.

There's much more to podcasting. If you are thinking of adding a podcast to your repertoire of "instruments" to help you build your business, read on. Here's some advice and insight from some of my successful podcasting friends who host my favorite podcasts.

Don Komarechka
*Photo Geek Weekly*
Audio-only, except for live episodes
Photogeekweekly.com

Starting a podcast is not for everyone. For years, I was happy to be a guest host on various platforms, opining on all subjects, from the latest advancements in technology to my own photographic expertise.

After a few years, I came to the realization that I wanted to have my own weekly soapbox. If no one listened, then I'd let the concept expire. It started small, with a few dozen people listening to the first episodes. The feedback was minimal, and I was mostly speaking to myself. I added a guest host after the first few episodes, and interest grew.

After fifty episodes, there was a reliable audience of roughly one thousand people. Now at over a hundred and fifty episodes, the weekly audience is over six thousand and growing rapidly. Momentum is found over time, consistency, and quality of content.

I've lost some episodes entirely due to technical failures. I've had to hire outside help to clean up the audio when a most excellent guest had incredibly poor audio. All the while, the podcast itself has not made me a penny. In fact, the hosting expenses have cost me a small sum every month for years. Still, there is value in having an audience that perceives the podcast as a sort of "one way friendship."

I love this—meeting people at conferences, workshops, or presentations and hearing that they are a fan of the podcast and my opinions. I feel a bit at a disadvantage since they know so much about my thoughts and I know none of theirs.

When I hold workshops, launch a crowdfunding endeavor, or ask for support in any of my professional activities, that friendship reveals itself. That loyal audience wants to give something back, and I am humbled by the sincere responses I get.

While the podcast itself does not have any sponsors, the audience itself is always worth building. I have made friends from the podcast when people are vocal about their differing, but valid, opinions. I have strengthened my network of contacts, I continue to hone my public speaking skills as a result of weekly recordings, and it brings me joy to geek out about photography, on or off the record.

As an addendum to this short piece I did for Rick's book: Apple is rolling out podcast subscriptions, which I think I will be exploring. I have roughly four thousand to five thousand listeners per week, and if a small portion of those listeners decides to pay $1 to $2 per month, that might amount to a mortgage payment. Not sure if your passive income tips will cover those areas, but there is also Patreon, which functions in a similar way.

Ant Pruitt
*Hands-On Photography*
Audio and video
www.twit.tv.hop

Getting up and running with podcasting is so easy. Anyone can do it these days. There's no need for a big, fancy studio or anything like that. You can literally record a podcast from your smartphone. It's *that* easy.

What's not easy? Consistency—the consistency needed to create a successful podcast. There are millions of podcasts created each year, but there are just as many podcasts that stop publishing each year. Why? There are a couple things to consider, but the majority of the time it has to do with the lack of consistency from the podcast producer. Recording the first episode is easy. Recording twenty episodes is not.

My advice to those interested in podcasting is to make an honest commitment to yourself and your target audience. Be you, know your content, and be ready to publish your content on a regular basis. Start with creating one episode, of course, but make a goal to create twenty episodes. As you approach twenty episodes, make a goal to create thirty episodes, and so on.

Like a finely tuned athlete or musician (like Mr. Sammon), you have to get the reps in. Practice, practice, practice, then publish. Over and over again.

As you get your reps, you will begin to grow your skills, you'll be able to create and publish more efficiently, as well as find your voice. It's rather a cliché for me to say, "be your authentic self," but there's truth in that statement. Your podcast should be *your* podcast, not a copycat of someone else's with their same tone and voice. Your audience will appreciate *that*.

The podcast road is long, and one should understand that long roads always have obstacles and challenges along the way. You may not have a huge audience starting out. That's okay. You may even receive negative feedback. That's okay, too. Continue to push forward.

On a personal note, as I began developing my podcasts for TWiT TV, I knew these challenges would be ahead. I've even had two shows cancelled due to lack of viewership. Sure, my ego was bruised, but only for a moment. I decided to turn that bruised ego into energy to get better at the craft as well as improve my other show.

Over a year of creating episodes every week, I've seen new milestones achieved. It's quite gratifying. No, I'm not a big, popular podcast host like the Joe Rogans of the world, but I'm proud to be the only Ant Pruitt of the world. The Ant Pruitt that continues to be himself, push himself, and help aspiring photographers get better at this awesome craft with bite-size tips and tricks.

Now, you do you. Go forth. Go create and dominate.

Ibarionex Perello
The Candid Frame
Audio only
www.thecandidframe.com

Consistency is key to having a successful podcast. It's important to understand that listeners are in a relationship with you when you are podcasting. Therefore, it's important to sustain and nurture that relationship by keeping your commitment to them to produce the best content possible on whatever schedule you've created for yourself and the show.

That's why it's important to be realistic about the work involved in producing a show, whether it's on a weekly, bi-weekly, or monthly schedule. As Rick mentions, don't underestimate the work involved, and be cognizant that a podcast is a long-term game. Though some podcasts may enjoy immediate success, most take time to ripen and find their audience.

Also remember that success is not measured solely by how many subscribers you have, but by the kinds of listeners who invest their time to listen to your show on a regular basis.

Always remember the motto: quality over quantity.

We talked about the cost in time of a podcast, but what about the financial cost? Well, for example, for the *Picturing Success* podcast, we used a company called Libsyn and we paid $20 or $25 per month (their plans are probably different now in 2021).

Larry is still paying $5 per month to keep those older shows available.

And speaking of shows, Larry and I recorded exactly two hundred shows. Multiply that by three hours and forty-five minutes per show, and you'll see why I needed to take a break.

Steve Brazill
Behind the Shot Podcast
www.behindtheshot.tv

If you ask ten podcasters this question: "What is a podcast?" you'll get ten different opinions. I've seen people debate this topic online to no end. Let me share my opinion. Of course, you are welcome to have your own. In fact, that's the beauty of podcasting!

Wikipedia defines a podcast as follows: "A podcast is an episodic series of spoken word digital audio files that a user can download to a personal device for easy listening."

That's a simplistic look at podcasts, but let's start there. Based on that definition, podcasts are a) episodic, and b) audio-only. I respectfully disagree with whoever wrote that.

I should probably clarify that my podcast is available in both audio-only and video versions. So yes, my opinion is colored by that fact, but I hope to share some insight into why I do video, and I will also share some of my stats to hopefully be as transparent as possible about my point-of-view.

When that definition says, "spoken word digital audio files," there is open debate on the topic of video as a podcast. Almost every definition or blog post I have seen has similar wording that singles out something like "digital audio file" or "audio program, like talk radio."

While most podcasts are audio-only, I would change this definition a bit. Let me explain.

A podcast is an RSS feed—a file that uses a standardized set of tags to identify a standard set of settings, and to reference media files stored online. RSS feeds can be subscribed to, which means they can provide the subscriber with notifications when the feed is updated, such as when a new episode is released. At its core, that's the end of the definition. Note that I didn't mention what type of media. Sure, it can be an audio file, such as an MP3, but it can also be a video file, like an MP4.

When I see people debate online that a podcast is audio-only, and video should just be put on YouTube, that is usually based on what a subscriber wants or will actually use. Most of the time podcasts *are* consumed as audio-only, that is true, but I would argue that part of the reason for that is simply because most podcasts don't have an RSS feed for video, they only put video somewhere like YouTube. So, what is a user to do if they prefer to "see" a show?

There are podcast apps that support video, in fact Apple Podcasts—
the app included on every iOS and MacOS device—supports subscrib-
ing to video shows.

The first podcast I subscribed to was *MacBreak Weekly*, from Leo
Laporte's TWiT network, and TWiT has a video feed for almost all of
its shows. I used to subscribe to both the audio-only and video feeds,
but over the years I found myself listening almost entirely to the audio-
only version. Periodically, I would check the video because I wanted to
see a specific topic or guest, but it was rare. Most of their shows are
tech news, and while the visual is nice, it's by no means required. My
show, on the other hand, definitely benefits from a video option.

On *Behind the Shot*, I sit down, virtually, with a photographer and dissect
how they made a photograph in pretty granular detail. That is easier to consume and understand if the audience can see the photo. For my audience,
there are a few options. They can listen to the audio-only version and
see the photo on the episode's blog post; they can watch the video wher-
ever they get their podcasts, assuming their service or app supports
video; or they can watch the video on my YouTube channel.

I've seen stats (through Edison Research via Podcast Insights) that suggest that 49% of podcast listening is done at home, and 22% of listening
is done while driving. Well, those people in the car should definitely
avoid video, but what about those at home? I have people share my
show often, showing them watching it on a big-screen TV. Perhaps, if
more video shows existed, then the audience for video might be bigger.

I've been asked why I put the video as a separate podcast feed, instead
of just using YouTube, and the answer might surprise some people.
First, it is more expensive to do video. There is the added equipment
for recording and editing, the bandwidth needed to maintain good
video quality for remote guests, and additional costs for the hosting,
where the actual files are stored. That said, there are some advantages,
for very specific use cases. For example, I don't want a large chunk of
my audience to be owned by YouTube. I control my feed, and my

audience knows where to find me. If anything happens to the YouTube feed, due to issues at YouTube, incorrect strikes against the account, or whatever, I still have an outlet established.

Additionally, viewing habits on YouTube are very different than podcast viewing/listening. The average view duration (AVD) stat on YouTube makes it clear that people want short-form videos, at least on YouTube. If you get an AVD of over ten minutes, you're doing pretty good I would think, although no stat is that simple. Mine is closer to fifteen minutes, but my shows are forty-five to sixty minutes long! People who subscribe in their app, knowing what the content is, are more likely to download my whole show. The last part of the puzzle is that the two are not mutually exclusive—it's just shelf space. My videos are on YouTube, if that's the way someone wants to consume them, but they're also available as a podcast in both formats.

I promised to share some stats, and I have to admit I was surprised by these numbers. Early on, I told people that about 50% of my podcast audience, not including YouTube, was listening to audio-only, and 50% was watching the video. Watching the stats for shows as they came in, I started changing that to 60/40, with the 60% being audio-only, but that was based on the fact that every episode was a bit different.

After Rick asked me to write about my podcast experience, I decided to use a wider sample of data. I downloaded my stats for the three most recent months, at the time of this writing, from March 1, 2021, through May 31, 2021, and also for the full year from May 2020 through May 2021.

Here is what I found: For the previous full year, audio-only listeners accounted for 57% of my downloads, while the remaining 43% were video. For the most recent three months, those numbers changed a bit with audio-only listeners accounting for 55% of my downloads, while the remaining 45% were video. So, the smaller, more recent sample shows that video viewing is up a little bit. Still, if 45% of my audience wants video, then they will get it the way they want to consume it.

In the end, podcasts are an easily accessible way for someone—

anyone—to create content. The beauty of podcasting is that it opens up a world that used to only exist in the corporate radio and TV stations arena to anyone with the gear and knowledge to self-publish, and they can create whatever their idea of good show might be.

One last thing: going back to that Wikipedia description, your podcast doesn't need to be "episodic," meaning each episode doesn't need to stand on its own, as with a news or current events type show, where the newest episode is listed first. You can also list a show as serial, meaning the episodes should be consumed in a specific order, like with a serial TV show. You may even choose to organize your podcast within seasons.

In other words, podcasts are just content, or shows and episodes, and they can be delivered in various ways.

Podcasts are a fun way to get your message or content out there. They are relatively easy and inexpensive to create, compared to what it might have taken even ten to fifteen years ago, and they can be very rewarding. That's not to say they aren't hard work. They can consume a lot of time, but if you've ever considered doing one, I say get started.

Make the show that *you* want to make.

**P.S** Here's a short list of some of the companies that host podcasts.

- Buzzsprout.com
- Captivate.com
- Castos.com
- Podbean.com
- Simplecast.com
- blubrry.com
- linksyn.com

# 11.

# RECORD AN ONLINE
# CLASS OR CLASSES

*"The beautiful thing about learning is nobody can take it away from you."*
—B.B. KING

Just about every photo pro I know, including pros who work for National Geographic, offers paid online classes. Some of these classes are offered on websites that offer many classes, such as KelbyOne.com (where I have recorded thirty classes), Lynda.com, and Master-Class.com. Some classes are offered on the photographer's website.

All classes are viewable worldwide (in most cases) 24/7. Again, that means you can make money while you are sleeping when someone is watching you "live."

The advantage to working with a company like KelbyOne is that folks who never heard of you, or folks who want to learn from the other photographers they follow, may find you and watch your class or classes. The disadvantage? Well, I really can't think of one, because it's in the website's best interest to promote you, make you look good, and sell your class or classes. Also, these established online companies have large audiences and inhouse marketing departments that package and promote your classes.

What's more, keeping in mind the "snowball effect" that I mentioned earlier in this book, the more classes you have on a website, the more views you will get, which translates into more passive income.

As I mentioned in the **Introduction**, payment varies from online training site to online training site, but I have seen the average class completion payment is between one and three thousand dollars, and the royalty payment (in addition to that payment) is a few dollars per-view per-class.

About the per-view per-class. Different companies work differently, but most companies require a viewer to watch most of the class before they make the payout. In other words, if a viewer only watches say 10–20% of the class, the instructor will not get paid for that view.

Considering that a typical photo class is about an hour and a half, investing the time in a class almost always leads to good Return on Investment. However, keep in mind that preparing for the class may take weeks or months. I usually spend about two months (part-time) preparing for a class.

The advantage to self-publishing an online class is that, if you have a big name, you may generate a greater percentage of profit per class. The disadvantage is that you need to produce, record, and edit the entire class yourself (or with your staff).

Plus, you'll need a server that lets viewers stream your class or classes without any lag whatsoever. In **Chapter 8: Offer a Downloadable PDF eBook**, I give a quick look at Content Shelf (contentshelf.com), a company I used that offers digital downloading services. SmugMug (smugmug.com) also offers video download capability.

In addition, you'll need to manage the class or classes, which may include making refunds and answering questions.

One of my good friends, Joel Grimes (joelgrimes.com), has produced many online classes that you can find on his website, and I encourage you to spend some time there. Following are his thoughts on the future of online education.

Take it away Joel.

You may have noticed that just about everywhere you turn, someone is selling online tutorial courses. This is especially true in the photography arena. If you wanted to sell your teaching courses, not too long ago, you had to go through venues like Lynda.com, KelbyOne, etc. But with the advent of web platforms such as Teachable, Kajabi, and Udemy, to name a few, it is relatively easy to build out your online courses or academy. And of course, creating content has gotten much more manageable these days with tools like GoPros, DJI Cosmos, iPhones, RØDE Wireless Go Mics, etc., and editing programs such as Final Cut Pro, Rush, and Camtasia.

Today's biggest challenge is not creating content or making it available to potential buyers, it is finding and targeting those buyers in a highly oversaturated market.

In the early days of my teaching, 100% of all my tutorial buyers were organic. Meaning, I picked them up through my social media outlets such as Facebook, Instagram, YouTube, and my photography website and blog. In addition to all the web exposure, I averaged around forty-five live speaking events a year, which allowed me to gain a loyal following.

Back in 2010, when I first started selling my tutorials online, my pricing guidelines were straightforward: one hour of content cost $100. With time, and as more photography educators began selling their content, one hour of content pricing began to drop drastically. Today, that same one hour of content goes for around $10. That means I have to sell ten times more tutorials to create the same income I did ten years ago.

To do that, I can no longer rely solely on my organic reach. The only other option I have is to pay for that reach. Online web-marketing in its simplest form is a numbers game. To effectively market online, you need a specialized, skilled team that knows exactly where to spend the money in order to gain the reach necessary to create a profit. It is next to impossible for one person to effectively generate the content, build out the online platform, and manage the ad spend. As a general rule, for every $1 of profit I generate today, I now need to spend around $3, which covers the web marketing team and, most importantly, the ad spend. In the future, my guess is that it will cost even more to generate the same amount of profit.

For future educators to compete in the online education marketplace, they can't do it alone and need to have a mindset that to create an income with their teaching, they have to pay to get the reach necessary for success. The problem is that this current model of marketing will exclude around 95% of all educators. This could be good or bad, depending on how you look at it. If you can create appealing content and hire a team to do all the web marketing and ad spend, you will fall into the 5% of educators that are rocking it in the online arena.

One final note, every three months, the online web marketing rules change. What works today will definitely not work down the road. This is why you need a specialized team to handle that side of things. To succeed, you often have to punt and start all over. This can be very frustrating and exhausting. If you are going to look at teaching to create an income, you have to implement a ten-year game plan. I have not met a successful online educator that did it in under five years. So be prepared to stick it out for the long haul.

Thank you, Joel. As an FYI, Joel has more than a dozen classes on his site, where he sells his classes exclusively.

There's another option for recording online classes: record the class yourself and let an established online training website offer your class. That is what my wife Susan and I did for two of my KelbyOne classes: *Uncovering the Magic of Utah's National and State Parks* and *Uncovering the Magic of Yellowstone and Grand Tetons*. We recorded the live videos (with my Canon digital SLRs and pro microphones), and then I inserted my photographs into those videos using iMovie. I also created a Keynote slide show for each class. I sent the finished movies to KelbyOne, they inserted an opener and a closer, and posted the videos to their site.

If you plan to go this route, it's important to talk with the training site to get specific recording settings. It's also important to send a test video, testing not only for video quality, but for sound quality as well.

As an aside, as strange as it may sound, sound can be more important in a video than the actual video.

Many of the tips that apply to the writing of a book (covered in **Chapter 7: Write or Narrate a Book**) apply to producing an online class. I'd suggest reading that chapter before this one.

As a brief recap, those elements (with a few word changes that apply to online classes) are:

- Study and know your subject, inside and out.
- Know where you are going.
- Respect the viewer.
- Leave no question unanswered.
- Know your competition.
- Have more material than you think you need.
- Make it easy and fun for the producer to work with you
- Let your personality show/shine through.
- Have fun.
- PR your class.

Here are some additional and specific tips for recording an online class.

**Say "Thank you."** Right up front, say "Thank you" to the student for joining you and for spending some time with you. Professional broadcast newscasters do this as a way of engaging the viewer in a friendly manner.

**Grab their attention.** In the first few seconds of your video, you want to capture the student's attention. Important techniques include using body language, as in using hand gestures while you are speaking. The opposite of this is what is called "a talking head," which is a turn-off to most people.

Being enthusiastic is important, too! Enthusiasm is contagious. If you are excited about what you are presenting, your viewers will be excited, too.

**Use an accessory camera.** Built-in computer cameras are okay, but accessory cameras are a better choice. They are sharper, can offer a wider or narrower field of view, and the ability to naturally blur the background (which looks much better and cleaner than a Skype blurred background).

Today I use a Canon mirrorless camera (EOS R) with 24–105mm zoom lens set at 24mm. Before that, I used a $50 Logitech webcam. I like the mirrorless camera/zoom lens set up because I can easily change the aperture to either blur the background or keep it in focus. I can also easily change the exposure compensation setting, which is necessary to ensure a good exposure when I switch between wearing a black shirt and a white shirt. That tiny detail affects exposure.

As to the camera placement, try to set it up at eye level. That way, the student will be seeing you eye-to-eye, which is more intimate than when someone is looking up or down at you.

**Get a good mic.** A good microphone is key to sounding good when recording an online class, and the closer the mic is to your mouth, the better the sound. There are hundreds of mics to choose from, but most pros I know use RØDE mics. Serious pros add a pop screen/filter to reduce "pops" between words.

While you are speaking, try to monitor your level of energy. If it starts to drop off, viewers may drop off watching your class. That's bad for two reasons: 1) you don't want to lose viewers, and 2) some online training websites don't pay a full royalty on a class if the viewer does not watch the entire class.

If you wear glasses, adjust your monitor and lights so they are not reflected in the camera. My solution: I don't wear glasses while I am recording.

**Have good lighting.** Indoors and out, lighting is important, so you look your best on camera.

Outdoors, shade, and overcast days produce soft and flattering light. If it's sunny, you'll want to be facing the sun, which may require wearing sunglasses. If you are side-lighted on camera, the hard light can be unflattering. What's more, getting an even exposure of you and the scene can be a bit tricky. If you are backlit, it will be hard to see your face.

Indoors, soft, and flattering light on your face is important, too. I am sure you have seen large ring lights advertised for being on camera at home. These lights can produce soft lighting, but you need to be careful of how the ring of light looks in your eyes. In some cases, it can look very weird. Ring lights can also create distracting reflections in eyeglasses.

Room light can be flattering, but it can change throughout the day if you don't have dark shades on your windows, as I do. Basically, you'll want your lighting to be consistent, that way you don't have to record at the same time every day—hence the dark window shades.

My suggestion is to carefully research the many different home lighting systems that are available, see if they are returnable, and then choose the one that makes you look your very best.

My lighting is simple and affordable. I use a combination of room light and standard table lamps placed behind my computer monitor. I experimented with different wattage bulbs so the lights from the lamps matched the light from the room lights.

**Shine but don't shine.** You want your personality to shine through on camera, but you do not want your face to look shiny. Makeup powder can help prevent "hot spots" on your face, especially on your forehead and nose. Honestly, I apply it every time I am on camera.

**Create a good background.** For sure, viewers will look to see what is in your background. Some look out of curiosity; others are interested to get a glimpse into your lifestyle. My best tip about a background: don't set up in your bedroom.

Another tip: make your background interesting, inviting, and friendly. For example, I have a few of my guitars in the background of my recording area, as well as several photographs on the wall. On my desk, I have a few of my books and a camera.

**Give an outline.** There's an old expression: "Tell them what you are going to tell them, tell them, and then tell them what you told them."

In other words, begin your class with a preview of what they are going to learn. Use the strongest images or videos you have. Then give your presentation, again using strong imagery to convey your point. Finally, do a recap. Again, the stronger your imagery, the more impact your class will have on your students.

**Have a call to action.** Having a call to action is always a good idea because it keeps the student engaged after your class is completed. The call to action I usually give is a self-assignment asking the students to put into practice what they learned. Another call to action I give is to meet up with other photographers and apply some of the newly learned techniques.

**Give your contact info.** Remember to tell folks where they can contact you.

In addition to that info, I *always* say, "You are a student for life. Don't be shy about contacting me by email and asking a question." That phrase does result in spending some time (while I am awake) answering some questions, but it pays off, because the follow-up emails usually result in additional class and book sales (which generate income while I am sleeping).

**Say "Thank you" again.** As simple as it sounds, "Thank you" means a lot to people. Gary Vaynerchuk talks about this in his book, *The Thank You Economy*, which was a #1 best seller on *The New York Times* books list.

In closing this section of this chapter, I'll say thank you for being here, and good luck with your recordings. I am rooting for you!

My good friend Larry Becker has recorded many online classes and is the master of ceremonies at many of the KelbyOne live online events. Larry wrote a wonderful book for those who want to look and sound their best on-camera. The book is called *Great on Camera* and it's available on Amazon.com.

Following is an excerpt from one of the chapters in Larry's book. I think this will help you produce the best possible online class.

## Take it away, Mr. Larry Becker!

As an on-camera presenter, you can and should use your knowledge of several subliminal body language cues, voice inflection styles, and actual words to influence your audience. But you should always do it in an ethical way, and never misrepresent yourself or your offer.

You send several categories of subliminal cues when you're on camera. When you know what you're doing on camera, some positive things you can convey include:

- Confidence
- A positive attitude
- Urgency
- Intelligence
- Likability
- Energy
- Excitement
- Believability
- Knowledge/expertise
- A calm mood

Keep in mind that you can convey the opposite of any of these characteristics too, and that's what you want to avoid. Being aware of the things you do on camera that make you appear nervous, shy, evasive, untruthful, dull, bored, angry, annoyed, or uneducated is good, professional practice. And unfortunately, many of these cues happen automatically to people who are nervous about being on camera.

What's worse, many negative cues happen just because of the filming style, lighting, or audio and can be beyond the direct control of the on-camera talent, especially if they don't know about it.

Looking at the list of positives you should convey you might have noticed that while a calm attitude and excitement are both positive, you probably can't convey them both at the same time. There may be an opportunity to be excited during part of your video and calm during some other part, but you don't have to convey all the positives all at once.

It's important to note here, that these are emotions and attitudes that you *appear to convey* by the overt and subliminal cues you give while on camera. They are not necessarily what you are really feeling in the moment. I make this distinction because so many people are overwhelmed by a sense of powerful nerves when they first start presenting on camera. But that's not the "real" you. That's not who you are in person. You aren't a nervous wreck with a wide-eyed, scared expression when you're talking with your friends in a casual situation.

You're not nervous when you're talking about the cool products and services your company provides. The goal is to use every tool in your arsenal to be more like the real, friendly, likable you when you're on camera.

One of the things that's a bit more of a subliminal "push" is to start explaining something you want the viewer to do, and nod affirmatively as you explain. You want your body language to signal that you are friends with the viewer, you already know that they're going to buy what you're selling, and then you just lead them positively through the buying experience. Slow, subtle, periodic positive nodding can lead viewers to think that their good feeling about you and your product/service are their own idea.

Asking questions is usually bad in videos. That's because

asking a question causes the audience to automatically go into a thinking process where they generate an answer. Sure, sometimes it's the answer you expect, but sometimes the mood of the viewer can be different than you expect, and they answer the question in a sarcastic way that automatically puts them in a mood that reduces your credibility and value in their eyes.

For example, the millennial generation tends to say, "Hey, what's up?" Or "Hey, how's it going?" as a casual conversation opener. Ironically, while they think it's cool, casual, friendly, and informal, it isn't interpreted by everyone in the same way. People my age, and even some millennials, think it's rude, disingenuous, dismissive, and even selfish to ask someone how they're doing and then totally ignore their response while continuing to talk about your own message. The only exception for this in my opinion, is when you do a live video. People actually can answer your question in the chat stream and then it's okay.

On the other hand, if you have walked through some level of an explanation about something and you're now approaching the call to action (CTA), where you ask somebody to go to a website or make a phone call, you can use tried and proven sales techniques. Asking a few questions where the obvious answer is "yes" puts the viewer in the frame of mind where they'll say "yes" a few times and then when you ask for the sale or encourage the CTA, they've said yes and then they're more likely to say yes again. But remember, this process should come after a bit of engagement and explanation on video. You can't use the 'yes questions' process on a cold viewer. It only works if somebody has engaged for a little while and "warmed up" to you and your offer.

If you're creating a video to sell or explain your products and services and it's a recorded video (not live), then testimonials and even simple scenes of people happily using your product send the signal of social proof. Nobody wants to be the first person to buy because they might be sold something that's really bad or worthless. Testimonials help people rationalize a positive feeling about your product because "Other people have bought it. They like it. I won't be the first."

But with modern social media, live videos change a few things. Livestream commenters can provide social proof that other people are interested too. You can answer questions. You can improve your explanations based on the questions you get. Viewers will feel better about themselves and like you a lot because of something as simple as a "shoutout."

In closing, before you go on camera, remember these five techniques:

- Smile. You'll look more likable and engaging.
- Use open-handed gestures and never point at the camera.
- Listen to your voice inflection and raise and lower your tone periodically.
- Use short words, contractions, and other things that make you sound conversational.
- And as Rick always says, "Have fun!"

# 12.

# OFFER A NEWSLETTER

*"Why waste a sentence saying nothing?"*
—SETH GODIN

In case you missed my friend Ian Plant's business advice earlier in this book, here's an excerpt that applies to this chapter: "The single smartest thing you can do to make money is to aggressively grow your email marketing mailing list."

The reason I reinforce that message here: you need readers for your newsletter, and the more the merrier, so to speak.

To begin, yes, a newsletter can be an effective sales tool. No, your newsletter should not look like a sales tool.

In other words, you can generate sales, as well as increase your customer base and subscribers, with a newsletter. However, if your newsletter comes across solely as, "Buy now, I'm selling this product or service," especially week after week or month after month, your newsletter will probably have the opposite effect.

The solution? Make your newsletter mostly educational, with a few products/services woven in and mentioning the benefits of those items. Of course, use strong images to grab the reader's attention. And, perhaps most importantly, make it personal and let your personality shine through.

Most newsletters by my photographer friends are free and I recommend that you offer a free newsletter, unless you have unique information and know of big product discounts.

My friend Joe Brady's (www.joebradyphotography.com) newsletter is a good example of a free personal and educational newsletter. Please allow me to analyze one of his newsletters for both our benefits. What follows is his basic format:

He has a nice and appropriate newsletter banner:

# FOTOFRIDAY

# A WEEKLY NEWSLETTER FOR

# FELLOW PHOTOGRAPHERS

Note the "fellow photographers," which immediately makes the newsletter friendly and makes the recipient a peer.

Under the newsletter banner (and logo) is his website (with a link):

# LAND, SEA & SKY

# JOE BRADY PHOTOGRAPHY

Joe usually starts off with a personal message, telling readers where he is on the planet and what he is doing. It's a fun read.

Then Joe offers a video tutorial, which says, "For you." At this point you have learned something for free, with no sales pitch.

Next, Joe talks about some of the gear that he uses, adding affiliate links, so if the reader buys the product, Joe makes a few "peanuts."

A note about peanuts: Joe's newsletter also mentions (from time to time) his photo workshops and tours, which, like all photo workshops, generate enough peanuts to feed more than a few elephants. It's a soft sell, and Joe's newsletter helps to keep him in mind when folks are looking for tours and workshops.

Taking a break from talking about my friend Joe Brady, I know another Joe whose newsletter is solely about going on his tours and workshops. He and his company go to exotic locations, and his prices are higher than the prices most photographers charge. Does his newsletter work for him? Probably so, but he has been around for a long time and has a large (and wealthy) client base who like to travel with him.

Okay, back to Joe Brady. Toward the end of his newsletter Joe goes back to making his newsletter personal, by adding a link to a free exercise video by his wife, Diane. Joe adds a link to Diane's YouTube channel and workout channel. If a reader likes the videos, they can take paid classes from Diane.

Closing each newsletter, Joe may share a book (not always on photography) that he is reading, and he always adds a personal note.

Like me, Joe uses Constant Contact (constantcontact.com) to design and e-mail his newsletter. Most of my photographer friends use Constant Contact, but there are many other services you can choose from and find by doing a Google search.

I like Constant Contact because designing an attractive newsletter is easy—you can choose from a wide array of templates. What's more, you can check to see how many folks actually opened your newsletter, which can help you determine if you are doing something right or wrong.

Constant Contact offers two pricing plans: Email (starting at $20/month) and Email Plus (starting at $45/month). Pricing variations are based on the account's number of email contacts. Discounts are available with upfront payment for 12 months (15% off).

In **Chapter 15: Get into Webinars**, I offered a suggestion for a closer. Here's that suggestion again. This can work for the close of your newsletter, too:

1) Give a call to action, perhaps a photo assignment.
2) Give away something for free.
3) Most importantly, give folks a reason to come back (in this case, to subscribe to your newsletter) and to follow you on social media.
4) Always say thank you!

**P.S.** I opened this chapter with this quote by Seth Godin: "Why waste a sentence saying nothing?" I use it again here to make an important point: If you have nothing new or interesting to put in a newsletter, there's really no reason to publish it.

What's more, you need to make a newsletter content plan weeks or months in advance of publication. Part of that plan should be to send out a newsletter on a weekly, monthly, or quarterly basis.

# 13.
## STRIVE FOR SPONSORSHIP

*"Once I took to Twitter and shared those jokes, they became a
huge hit. My following grew, and some of the posts got
thousands of retweets. With so many shares,
money from sponsors followed."*
—VIRENDER SEHWAG

All the successful photographers I know have sponsors. Some
have only a camera sponsor; others have camera, software,
plug-in, photo service (like printing), memory card, camera
store, lighting, and camera bag sponsors. Some have travel company
sponsors, too.

These sponsorships generate passive income, but there is no such
thing as a free lunch. While you are awake, you need to promote your
sponsor's products and services on social media, in personal appearances, and so on.

To get a sponsor, you need a good reputation, a "name," and a large
following on social media. Most companies want a photographer to
have at least 100,000 follows on a single social media site.

As an aside, as strange as it may sound and as wrong as it may sound, you don't have to be a good photographer to have a large following on social media. Being a good marketer, having a good look, a unique look, and being a bit "crazy" and "out there" are all qualities that have helped folks gain large followings on social media.

Well-known athletes make tens of millions of dollars on sponsorships, some of which they invest so they can make money while they are sleeping.

Sponsorships for well-known photographers vary from company to company and from photographer to photographer. Generally speaking, sponsorships include enough much-appreciated cash and/or gear to help photographers pursue their passion.

Some companies offer a contract-signing payment plus a per-project (like a speaking engagement) payment, while other companies offer some gear and/or a discount on gear.

Some photographers I know get their sponsorship in gift cards from online camera stores—they get a monthly gift card, for say $500 a month, that they can redeem only at the camera store. So, the $500 saves the photographer $500, but the camera store is not really spending $500 on the photographer, because he or she is buying products from the store.

But again, there is no free lunch. Sponsors expect their photographers to deliver, especially on social media. Stop delivering and the sponsorship stops.

Another advantage of having a sponsor is that the company promotes you to a much larger audience than you have. The sponsor helps you to increase your reach and your audience. Sponsorship also enhances your reputation, especially when that sponsor is a major camera company.

Earlier in this chapter, I mentioned travel company sponsorships. Again, each deal is different. Sometimes, you get a free trip with all expenses paid in exchange for promoting the company on social media and perhaps being an on-site photo pro. Sometimes a day rate is added.

And yes, again, you need to deliver. If you don't, you will not be invited back. What's more, many travel companies and tour operators know each other. If you don't deliver for one company and approach another company, your reputation may precede you.

When it comes to sponsors, you need to be up front. On my website, I have a Sponsors page. Most pros I know do the same.

If you skipped ahead to this chapter and missed **Chapter 3: Socialize or Succumb**, check it out. In that chapter, I talk about, among other things, how to make your sponsors happy, which is key to keeping them.

# 14.

# CREATE CONTENT FOR A YOUTUBE CHANNEL

*"The great thing about YouTube is there are no gatekeepers.*
*No one is waiting to tell you if you're good enough.*
*It's just your audience."*
—LINDSEY STIRLING

nyone can have a YouTube channel, and that includes you.
Anyone can monetize their YouTube channel (get accepted
into the AdSense program) with a few caveats:

- You need to have more than 4,000 watch hours (total time spent watching any of your videos) in the past 12 months.
- You need to have more than 1,000 subscribers.
- Your channel must be linked to a Google AdSense account.
- You must follow YouTube's monetization policies, including community guidelines and AdSense program policies.

To get started monetizing your YouTube channel, go to your channel, click on YouTube Studio and then on Monetization. However, before you do that, you should do this web search: "Monetize your YouTube channel". You will find that it's relatively easy to set up, but it does take time.

And speaking of time, while you are awake, you really do need to put in the time to post videos if you want to make passive income.

How much can you make? Well, as with all the questions I am asked, it depends. Here it depends on the number of videos, the number of views, and interestingly enough, where the viewers are based. So, building an audience—discussed in **Chapter 3: Social or Succumb**—is über important.

As a basic guideline, you may make between $1 and $2 per 1,000 views. I know those are peanuts, very small peanuts, but if you build your brand and viewers, those peanuts add up, so read on!

My advice to YouTube photo creators is to make your channel fun and engaging, as well as educational. For example, on my Rick Sammon YouTube channel, when I post something that's educational, I also try to make it fun. What's more, I also post solely fun videos, including videos I made of an elephant in Botswana licking my face, a tuk-tuk ride through the streets of India, and several guitar jam sessions. On the Photo Therapy YouTube channel, I post slide shows of the members' photographs along with original piano compositions.

When creating your YouTube channel keep in mind that it may be the first time someone is actually seeing you. Remember that first impressions are important (Larry Becker talks about this in **Chapter 11: Record an Online Class or Classes**).

One talented photographer I know, PhotoJoseph (www.youtube.com/pho-tojoseph), spends a lot of time creating YouTube videos. At the time of this writing (summer 2021), he has 65K subscribers, and one of his videos has more than 24K views.

You may not be a PhotoJoseph, but you can aspire to have a following like him.

Here's a bit of his inspiring story and advice, in his own words.

> Hey readers, I'm PhotoJoseph. I've known Rick for long time, following him throughout the growth of my own career, and it's an honor to be part of this book.
>
> I got into photography at a very (very) young age but deviated from the path to go corporate for the first big part of my career. When I finally took the leap to go independent, I figured out pretty quickly (and painfully) that the best way to make this last was to have diversified income. Rick talks about this in the Preface to this book: Don't put all your eggs in one basket.
>
> Relying on a corporate paycheck is scary enough—even if it comes from a multi-billion-dollar company—because it can vaporize in an instant. But if you're your own boss and still living job to job, you could be just one 'no' from missing a rent payment. That's some scary stuff too.
>
> As Rick will tell you throughout this book, there are (at least!) two things that you need to build your safety net: diversification, and passive income. Following his father's mantra of "It takes a lot of peanuts to feed an elephant," you absolutely want

money—even small amounts of it—trickling in from as many sources as possible. And just as important, you want those trickles to come in even when you are not working. While you're sleeping. While you're watching TV. While you're hanging out with friends and family.

I'll never forget the first 'ping' of my very first eBook sale, my first $20 electronic sale and delivery. I wasn't even at my desk; I was out in the desert scouting locations for a photography workshop. I wasn't getting paid to be out in that desert, but I got paid. And I didn't have to lift a finger. The fingers had already been lifted and were now busy doing other things. That $20 changed my life.

Jump forward ten-plus years, and about half of my income is passive. Some of it comes from my monetized YouTube channel; both from advertisements and affiliate sales revenue (I get dozens of affiliate checks per month—some are just a few peanuts, but those peanuts add up).

Some of it comes from memberships and sales on PhotoJoseph.com. Some of it comes from video training I did for Lynda.com, and then LinkedIn Learning. There's an ever-trickling flow of peanuts making their way into my bank account.

The other great thing about having a presence on YouTube, and social media in general, is branding. You'll hear this a lot: Build your brand.

Your brand is you. That's 100% true, and super-important to remember. Everything you do is a reflection of yourself and your brand, and when you do awesome work on any visible platform (for me that's largely YouTube), that's a great way to be seen. Most of my best paying commercial work these days comes from companies that found me on YouTube, like my style, and ask me to make videos for their products and services.

Of course, not every experiment will work. But building passive income gives you the freedom to try different things without worrying whether or not it'll work. Some do, some don't, and that's okay. It's hard in the beginning to put a lot of work into something that you know might only make you $100 a month. I totally get that. But do one here and there. Eventually they add up.

"For more learning, check out my online presence, starting with_my YouTube channel. You can also find me by typing "PhotoJoseph" into any social media platform you like. Odds are that you'll find me rather quickly. See what I do, and how I do it. Ask me a question on Twitter. Drop a comment on a YouTube video. Be a part of the conversation. And I'll see you online.

Good luck and have fun other there.

Before going on, I want to thank PhotoJoseph for taking the time to share his thoughts on the theme of this book: making money while you are sleeping.

There are more ways to make a few bucks on YouTube, including selling paid content, promoting a product or service, licensing your content to other companies, and channel memberships.

Monetizing your YouTube channel, however, is not for everyone. My friend and podcaster Steve Brazill (behindtheshot.tv) explains why:

> First, at around 5,000 subscribers, it's not that big. More important, each episode is about someone else's photo. I don't monetize because it's possible that someone would be upset by my monetizing from their content. Plus, I'd need a signed release for each show, which really complicates things. I do monetize videos that are reviews or conference recaps, but that's maybe four or five videos, which is pennies. But as Rick says, all those

pennies/peanuts add up.

Anyway, that's the main thing: I'm not comfortable making money from other people's content. I'd also have to be sure to change each video to say it contains someone else's copyright.

Another one of my friends, Don Komarechka also does not monetize his YouTube channel. He says, "I really wish I had more time to build my YouTube channel! It's not something I actively pursue right now. Most of my videos appear on YouTube channels owned by others, including the videos I paid to create for DPReview TV."

Like Steve and Don, I don't monetize my YouTube channel. Rather, I spend time creating content for KelbyOne.com. I have recorded more than thirty-one hour-plus classes for that platform. I did the math—time and payments—and for me, KelbyOne was the way to go.

If you think monetizing a YouTube channel is in your future, I'd suggest doing some research before you start recording. Your research could begin by reading one of the many books on Amazon about making money with a YouTube channel.

**P.S.** PhotoJoseph and Steve Brazill are awesome photographers and podcasters, and I recommend that you follow them. Another most-excellent photographer/podcaster, one who also has a large following on YouTube, is my friend Nick Page (www.nickpagephotography.com). Watch and learn from Nick, too. You'll enjoy the process.

# 15.

## GET INTO WEBINARS

*"Tell me and I forget, teach me and I may remember,*
*involve me and I learn."*
—CHINESE PROVERB

For sure, there's money to be made in producing webinars. Folks can watch even after your live broadcast, perhaps while you are taking a nap.

Basically, you have a choice of producing a free or a paid webinar. But here's the thing, you can also make money by doing a free webinar, and you may even make more. Here's why: there is so much free stuff out there today that many people are resistant to pay for a webinar no matter how much they'd like to attend, and as affordable as it may be.

So, naturally, a free webinar on the same topic as a paid webinar will attract more people. So how do you generate income? First, by establishing credibility as an expert that the viewer can trust. Second, by offering, in a subtle way, paid stuff: maybe a book, a class, a workshop, a tour, a seminar, a PDF and so on. What's more, if you offer that stuff at a discount (everyone loves a discount), you may end up generating a bigger profit than you would if you sold the same stuff at full price.

Here's an example: I've done free webinars on traveling to Antarctica for Abercrombie & Kent, a world leader in luxury travel. As an A&K photo coach I talk about photographing in Antarctica, and then an A&K executive talks about the expedition in general. The goal of these webinars is to get people to travel with A&K to Antarctica and to come home with great pictures.

These webinars work for A&K, and I've met people on the expeditions who come on my own photo workshops and tours. Some folks also buy my books. Working on the webinars has helped me market my products and services to a wider audience.

Free webinars are good for everyone. And because viewers see you giving away free stuff, including valuable information, you can come across as a good person, as long as you keep your sales pitch subtle.

Producing a good webinar is similar to producing an online class, something I talk about in **Chapter 11: Record an Online Class or Classes.** If you haven't read that chapter and want to do webinars, I strongly recommend you take an especially long look at what Larry Becker says about looking good on camera, as well has having a good set, a good camera, and a good microphone. Equally important is a basic "script" that will help you keep on track and ensure that you get your "copy points" across to your viewers.

So far in this book, I've mentioned and quoted my dad several times. Here's part of a conversation we had after he saw that I was giving free webinars and posting free stuff on YouTube:

Dad: "Rick, why are you giving so much stuff away when you could be charging for it?"

Me: "The more I give away, the more I make."

What I told my dad was basically what I outlined above.

Once again, if it works for me, it can work for you as long as you keep in mind that content is king and that you must always respect the viewer.

Thanks to helpful websites, setting up a webinar is easier than it used to be. Most folks I know use GoToWebinar (gotowebinar.com) and those who charge get paid through Eventbrite.

Oh yeah, don't forget to test everything—including sound, screen sharing, and room lighting—well in advance of your live event. After a successful test where you've successfully ironed out the kinks, don't change anything. The idea is not to have any technical variables.

In closing, I'd like to give you four tips for closing your webinar.

1) Give a call to action, perhaps a photo assignment.
2) Give away something for free.
3) Most importantly, give folks a reason to come back and to follow you on social media.
4) Always say thank you!

# 16.

## SELL PRINTS ONLINE

*"I don't care if you make a print on a bathmat, just as long as
it is a good print."*
—EDWARD WESTON

This chapter is one of my favorites in this book, because three of
The All-Star Photo Marketers—Karen Hutton and Jonathan
& Angela Scott—share some valuable advice for selling prints
online and I love listening to them.

It's such good advice, in fact, that after I finish writing this book, I
am going to look into selling prints online. Right now, I only sell prints
that I print myself, a process I thoroughly enjoy. It also gives me 100%
creative control, and I can manually (as opposed to digitally) sign and
number each print.

However, I can't do it while I'm asleep. Speaking of keeping me up,
packing and shipping prints also takes away from my nap time, as does
speaking with customers about orders.

My technique for selling hand-printed editions: On each page of the
Galleries on my website/store, I have box: Prints for Sales. Contact

ricksammon@mac.com. I also have a page on my website, Prints for Sale that shows my price list.

If you are interested in selling prints online, which, as Karen Hutton points out, "is a ton of work in the beginning," I think this chapter is for you.

## Karen Hutton

I've had a camera in my hands almost my entire life. My heroes were Ansel Adams, Edward Weston, Minor White, Paul Caponigro, and others of that era. My dream from the very beginning was to sell beautiful prints on amazing materials. In other words, fine art.

As life would have it, my career took off in other directions—teaching, traveling, leading photographic retreats, speaking, and brand partner collaborations.

I loved it all, and I still do! But the fine-art dreams? They consistently took a back seat. Sure, I sold prints along the way, usually large format ones, but it wasn't my focus; it was simply a by-product of everything else I was doing. And yet, I looked at those moments as a sort of proof-of-life that kept the dream alive.

The year of COVID-19 wiped the slate clean in one fell swoop. Disappointing? You bet. But I also saw it as an opportunity to lean into fine art at long last.

That happened in two ways:

1. I developed an entirely new line of art that I call "Whimsical Reveries," borne out of the intense introspection and exploration of 2020.

2. Turning my focus at last to the one thing that started me on my photographic journey in the first place: creating and selling fine art photography, creating installations, collaborating on projects that needed my brand of visual storytelling.

As a lifelong entrepreneur, one thing I've learned is to always have multiple streams of income, which is what Rick also recommends. As a photographic creative, that might mean writing, teaching, speaking, brand partnerships, commercial projects, portraits, weddings, or whatever avenues suit one's unique talents and interests.

In my case, I still teach (online), speak (online), write, collaborate on projects, maintain brand partnerships and now, finally, I create/sell fine art prints.

I love my in-person collaborations and installations, which I'm blessed to be doing again.

But if there's one thing the year of COVID-19 taught us all is that selling art online is a crucial avenue to include! The art world did indeed experience a shift of epic proportions, with galleries and museums closing (some temporarily, some permanently), and losing millions of dollars of revenue.

What took its place? Online sales. Even the staunchest, old-school galleries figured out some way to do it, much as it pained many to do so. The consensus: even as in-person sales are picking up again, online art sales are here to stay.

The best part for artists? It opened up a massive opportunity. The fact that artists could take their destiny and sales into their own hands, and build their own following, client base, and business and income stream meant a whole new world transformed before our eyes.

**Here's why I do it:**
1) It puts the power and control of my destiny into my own hands.
2) Whether I succeed or fail is all up to me.
3) While it's a *ton* of work, especially in the beginning, it's also a way to experience that much-sought-after passive income. Let's be clear though: it's only passive in the sense that you can wake up in the morning to new sales transpiring while you slept. Because creating those sales is anything *but* passive!
4) I can tell my story, my way—to a much broader audience. The online aspect of fine art presentation offers a variety pack of opportunities: social media, live broadcasts, self-made or

professional videos, writing about my work, doing all kinds of fun events and seasonal or spot sales, giveaways, sharing "extras" with my email subscribers. All of these offer ways to connect with and reach people in my own unique way. I love connecting, and I love creating a "world" where people can come and feel good, enjoy spending time, have a laugh, walk away feeling uplifted, and perhaps with a bit more $O_2$ in their souls. I refer to my work as "Oxygen for Your Walls," you see. It's all part of my "why" for creating art in the first place. Always has been.

5) Giving back. I've always given back in real-time, to my people, in person. But working online is offering new ways to do that. Better still: it blends my love for fine art with helping others in truly unique ways.

**Here's how I do it:**

1) Websites. For the variety of avenues in my business (besides art/photography/teaching/speaking (I also do voiceovers professionally), I need more than one website. Each one is a specialist, offering the best tools for the job I require. As of this writing, here's how it works:

- Karenhutton.com is the portal to my world and is built on WordPress. Voiceovers, teaching, upcoming events, etc.—you can get to any of my tracks from there.
- KarenHuttonArt.com is my fine art print gallery and shop. Open editions, limited editions, custom prints—I can offer them all in one place. It's built on Art Storefronts (artstorefronts.com). Their tools and features are all geared specifically toward fine-art sales—clients can even use Live View with Augmented Reality to see how art looks in their space or use a selection of rooms where they can change rooms, wall colors, etc., to get an idea of how it will look. Between that and their tech and marketing

support, it's the best place for my fine-art online presence.

- **KarenHuttonPhotography.com** is my photo portfolio site. It serves the collaboration, installation, and projects work I do directly with clients. As such, it's the service-based (vs. product-based) segment of my business. That site is built on SmugMug (smugmug.com). To me that's their specialty and where they excel since the backend they provide is second-to-none and my images look incredible there.

2) Social media for connection and marketing. Platforms morph and change, but right now, I focus more on Instagram, with its rich set of tools in Reels, IGTV, LIVE broadcasts, Stories, etc. I like one-stop shops. Overall, social is a great way to find *new* members of your audience who are just waiting to discover you. And it's another way to connect with existing followers who like to know what you're up to and what's new.

3) Newsletters. I value personal connection, as well as offering those who take the chance with me some extra goodness. I think of them as my "Insiders' Club," and enjoy finding fun ways to educate, inspire, and share new art and adventures. *Note:* You can create "Behind the Scenes" videos, include new work and your thoughts about how and why you created it, and even create educational videos about your work, and then share it all with subscribers. Invite the world to join! Your subscriber list is pure gold. Take good care of them and they'll be your best ambassadors the world over!

4) Events, especially virtual ones. The online world offers wonderful opportunities to show your work, sell it in real time, and connect with your audience through live events, charity events, and just about any other kind of celebration or event you can think of to build around your art sales.

**Karen Hutton**
www.karenhutton.com
Photographer, Artist, Purveyor of Awesomeness

# Jonathan & Angela Scott

Shortly after we launched our fine art collection, the world experienced a massive shift as a result of the COVID-19 pandemic. With galleries temporarily closed, world travel paused, and live events postponed, we were forced to re-evaluate our strategy for sharing our artwork and shift to a mostly online model. After a year of selling our fine art photography online, we're excited to share our tips for generating passive income through online print sales.

**Identify the Best Tools & Partners.** As with all online businesses, the processing of payments, production of products, and fulfillment of orders can be a very challenging and complicated process. When you begin setting up the infrastructure to sell your artwork online, our biggest tip is to find the best tools and partners to streamline the process.

By using a robust e-commerce platform—Shopify—we were able to simplify the process of accepting payments and processing orders, while also gaining access to basic analytics. After countless hours of searching, we were also able to identify a printing partner with the ability to seamlessly print and fulfill our international print orders. We even found a Shopify integration—Change Commerce—which allows our customers to seamlessly donate a portion of their purchase to a specific non-profit organization. The use of automation tools such as Shopify and Change Commerce has allowed us to save time, streamline our operations, and identify ways to grow the business.

**Share the Stories Behind Your Work.** By selling prints exclusively online, unfortunately you miss out on some of the more traditional ways people interact with artwork and engage with artists. For instance, there may not be physical galleries where customers can see and experience your artwork. Secondly, you may not have walk-in exhibitions or events, where there's usually an opportunity to share more of the passion behind your photography and engage with potential customers face-to-face.

For these reasons, we found that sharing stories through virtual channels is a very important aspect of our fine art photography marketing strategy. For example, with the launch of our gallery website, we also launched a YouTube channel. Here, we share "Behind the Shot" video stories that provide subscribers with more insights behind each photograph—what happened that day, the story behind the animal/location, how we visualized it, etc.

Another aspect of our photography is giving back to conservation. With donate 10% of each sale of our prints directly to a conservation organization that we believe in. For that reason, we have also tried to tell stories about the organizations and causes that our fine art photography supports. For example, we'll focus our content on a particular theme (i.e., World Cheetah Month) so as to share more conservation stories and raise awareness.

**Jonathan & Angela Scott**
The Jonathan & Angela Scott Collection, curated by David & Tori Scott, on www.thuranima.com.

Prints are also available on www.bigcatpeople.com.

**Rick here:** Fine Art America (www.fineartamerica.com) is another website that offers online photo sales, and more—from t-shirts to throw pillows, and from coffee cups to, believe it or not, shower curtains.

You can also sell prints (and lots of other stuff) on Instagram via the Instagram Shopping Cart.

# 17.

## LAUNCH AN
## ONLINE FORUM

*"Discussion is an exchange of knowledge; argument an
exchange of ignorance."*
—ROBERT QUILLEN

This is the shortest chapter in this book. In fact, you can look at
it as a long P.S. to the chapter on starting a Facebook group
because a forum is similar to a private Facebook group.

One difference is that you will attract people who don't like Facebook
for one reason or another. I know this, for sure, because I receive many
emails from folks who don't like Facebook and say that is the reason
why they are not joining the Photo Therapy group.

Another difference, and an advantage, to a forum is that you can set
up individual topics where folks can quickly post and comment on photographs and other comments, and easily find those by typing in a topic
in the Search field. You can add a topic to a post in a Facebook group,
but as I have found in my Photo Therapy group, topics are not that
easy to find. Also, when you open a Facebook group page, you see the

posts in the order in which they were posted.

Yet another difference is that a forum can be more personal. I have found this with the KelbyOne forum, also called the KelbyOne Community. KelbyOne members *love* being part of this community because, among other reasons, basically the rules are to be nice. The rules are "enforced" by a team of dedicated moderators. Another reason is that you can get alerts when folks comment on your photographs or posts.

We have moderators, twelve in fact, for the Photo Therapy Facebook group. We have the same philosophy: our group is a safe and fun place to share photographs and ideas.

If you decide to start and run a forum, a noble goal would be to build your audience and brand—and to keep sales pitches to a minimum. As I mention in **Chapter 15: Get into Webinars**, you may actually sell more stuff by not trying so hard to sell stuff.

I would suggest making a commitment to be very active in your forum, which is the same for a Facebook group. I probably spend more than an hour a day commenting on the members' photographs and comments in the Photo Therapy group. I also spend time approving or declining members. Our moderators have made a similar commitment. In fact, the group would not exist and continue to grow were it not for them. So, that's right, invite people you trust to be moderators.

All these "pluses" of a forum are not free to the person or group who sets up the forum. The cost to set up a forum can be up to a couple of hundred dollars a month. There is no cost to be a member of the forum.

If you are interested in starting a forum, here are a few of the online forum hosting sites:

- Discourse (Discourse.com)
- Vanilla (Vanillaforums.com)
- XenForo (xenforo.com)
- Invision Community (Invisioncommunity.com)

# 18.

## SUGGEST A PRODUCT TO A COMPANY

*"No amount of skillful invention can replace the essential element of imagination."*
—EDWARD HOPPER

As a preface to this chapter, here are a few words of encouragement: As you will read, being a well-known professional photographer is key to getting your name on a product. If you are not a top pro right now, please keep this photo adage in mind: All top professionals were amateurs at one time. And that includes me!

Suggesting a product to a company, and then having them develop it for and with you can be an effective way to generate income while you are sleeping. What's more, you don't need to make a financial investment, an investment that most photographers could not afford without the help of crowdfunding. I cover crowdfunding in **Chapter 9: Join the Crowd with Crowdfunding.**

I did this years ago with two products: Rick Sammon's On-Location Light Control Kit by Westcott (a reflector and diffuser kit in a small tote bag) and Rick Sammon's Sling Camera bag by Adorama (a small camera bag that slings over your shoulder).

Westcott basically repackaged products they already had in stock, and Adorama sewed my name on an existing bag and added a pocket.

The deal was profitable for all of us. Because the companies took the risk, they made most of the profit which was totally okay with me.

I also loaned my name to a series of my favorite digital photo frames— Rick Sammon's Favorite Frames—for On1 software. I received a small commission on each download. However, when the company was sold several years ago, I was pleasantly surprised at the truckload of peanuts that arrived after my buyout.

Hint: Work with software companies to develop styles, textures, backgrounds, and so on, if you really want to make a few bucks.

Yes, you need a big name, and a good name, if you want a company to work with you on a product. Social media can help you build a name and build a brand, as can hard work, combined with a passion for your craft.

If you don't have a big name yet but you have a great idea, a company may buy the idea from you.

And here's another possibility: a company may discover you, love your work, and come to you with a product development and endorsement idea.

Following is one of the best examples of how a pro works with a company. Joe McNally is one of the most well-known and respected photographers

I know. He is also a heck of a nice guy. Joe works with Manfrotto on his Signature Range lighting products. At last count, these are the products I found in Manfrotto's Joe McNally Signature Range:

- Joe McNally Skylite Rapid Diffuser with Masks
- Joe McNally Ezybox Speed-Lite 2 Plus
- Joe McNally Lastolite Ezybox Hotshoe
- Joe McNally Lastolite 4-in-1 Umbrella
- Joe McNally Lastolite UpLite Kit
- Joe McNally Collapsible Ironworks background
- Joe McNally Triflash.

Here's another example: Scott Kelby, head of KelbyOne.com and an excellent photographer (and a friend of mine and Joe's) has a product called the Westcott Learning Light, a kit that allows users to experiment with various lighting techniques without the need for complex or expensive equipment.

And one more product from a pro: My friend Joel Grimes designed the 24-inch Beauty Dish Switch for Westcott.

So, put on your thinking cap. You never know what product may be attractive to a company.

Finally, don't be afraid to pitch ideas and get rejections. Rejection is part of the entrepreneurial process.

# 19.
## TAKE STOCK OF STOCK PHOTOGRAPHY

As recently as the early 1990s, I knew photographers who were making more than $100,000 a year selling stock photography. One friend licensed a 35mm slide of a high-flying bald eagle with a fish in its talons to a German company for $18,000.

Today, in 2021, you can buy a high-resolution digital file of a bald eagle with a fish in its talons from iStock (istockphoto.com) for under $18.

Another photographer I know told me he bought a brand-new Mercedes Benz with the money generated from one month's worth of stock sales. Again that was back in the early 1990s. I trust and respect this photographer so I don't think he was exaggerating.

The world of stock photography has changed, no doubt. But as the saying goes, "When you are though changing, you are through." That saying applies to virtually every aspect of photography—and of course life. Changes bring opportunities, and opportunities are what photographers need to grow their business.

I'm not an expert on selling stock photos, but I am skilled at finding experts who can share their expertise with my readers.

To get some insight in selling stock photos, I reached out to **Mat**

**Hayward, Adobe Stock evangelist.**

Take stock in what he says. Take it away, Mat!

Photographers, videographers, and illustrators have a fantastic opportunity to monetize their work by putting it in front of the millions of Adobe customers around the world using Adobe Stock.

Adobe Stock is a traditional stock photography agency working as a free-standing site (stock.adobe.com) and is incorporated into Adobe applications such as Photoshop and Premiere Pro. Customers can purchase a license to use your work and that can provide a passive revenue stream that can flow for years.

You don't need an Adobe Creative Cloud subscription to become an Adobe Stock Contributor. The only requirement is an active Adobe ID (email address) to sign up.

If you are a Creative Cloud member, you can use the same Adobe ID to create your Adobe Stock Contributor account. You can upload your work directly through Adobe Bridge, Photoshop Lightroom, and Lightroom Classic.

To get started, visit the Adobe Stock Contributor portal: contributor.stock.adobe.com.

There are many tutorials online that show you the specifics of how to upload your content, so be sure to check them out if you are uncertain of the process. I'm going to provide you with some practical advice on how best to establish a solid portfolio with consistent sales.

# 10 QUICK TIPS:

- Emphasize space for copy
  - Leave room for designers to add text to your image when possible.
- Submit the maximum file size your camera can create

- Minimum file size is 4MP, though many customers filter based on size expectations/requirements so you could be leaving money on the table if you unnecessarily downsize your photos
- Seek alternative angles and provide customers with options
- Keep it real
  - Customers are looking for real looking people in real situations. Authenticity is key in today's world of stock photography.
- Stay up to date on current events
  - Watch the news. If you see something big is happening, try to capture it in a way that can be used commercially.
- Submit the best of the batch
  - Be selective and ensure each image you submit provides unique value to customers. If you are shooting 20 frames per second of a static pose with little difference, that is not 20 unique stock images.
- Representation
  - People want to see themselves represented in advertisements and other visual media. We live in a diverse world. Do your best to represent your interpretation of diversity and to be as inclusive as you can in your work.
- Plan for seasonal events
  - Customers are typically buying seasonal content 2–3 months in advance of the event/season. Don't submit Christmas images on December 26, for example. Shoot some stock under the tree, for example, but save it and upload it during the following October so customers can more easily find it when they need it.
- Less is more when it comes to post-processing.
  - Avoid filters, borders, etc. Submit the clean, sharp, color version of your photos to give customers the most

flexibility. For example, if a customer wants your photo in black and white, it's relatively easy for them to make the conversion themselves. The reverse isn't always true.

⚙ Shoot what you love

- Adobe reaches a wide stock content buying audience. With that diverse group of customers comes an equally diverse need for content. If you shoot it, there is likely an audience for it. Start with your passion and learn what sells for you. Continue to evolve and expand your portfolio.

## KEYWORDS COUNT, AND OTHER THINGS TO KNOW

You can submit the best photo in the history of the camera to Adobe Stock, but if a customer isn't able to find it, they won't buy it. It's up to you to help them find it. The most effective way to do this is through accurate, descriptive keywords and titles. Before you submit your work to Adobe Stock, you must add between five and forty-nine keywords (fifteen to twenty-five is usually the sweet spot). It is very important to note that the Adobe Stock search engine puts an emphasis on the first ten keywords you add. Make sure you list the most important and relevant keywords in the top ten!

You must also add a title describing the image before you can submit it. The title should read like a sentence. Words listed in the title are also searchable so be sure they count. It's encouraged to duplicate words that are listed in the title in the top ten keywords for added weight in search. Adobe Sensei will recommend up to twenty-five keywords and a title for you automatically if you do not embed the metadata prior to upload. Be sure to review the auto-keywords for accuracy. Remove anything that may be irrelevant, move the most important keywords to the top ten, and add anything you think may be missing.

If your image contains recognizable people or property, you must submit a signed model or property release with the file. Recognizable doesn't just mean a face when it comes to people. There are plenty of other ways to identify a person including a tattoo, scar, unique hairstyle, etc. When in doubt, get a release signed.

Once you've submitted your images, the Adobe Stock moderation team will review your content to make sure the quality standards have been met or exceeded and that there are no intellectual property violations. Watch out for trademarked logos or brand elements. The licenses being distributed through Adobe Stock are for commercial use, so trademarked content will always result in a rejection.

The intent is for your content to be approved and made available for sale. However, rejection happens to even the best photographers from time to time so don't take it personally. Possible rejection reasons are if the image is out of focus, has exposure issues, has excessive noise, etc.

The ideal result is that your photo is approved upon review. After approval, it is online and available in your portfolio for Adobe Stock customers to purchase a non-exclusive license to use. When a customer purchases a license for your work, you earn a royalty, paid into your Adobe Stock contributor account. The rate for images is 33% and the rate for videos is 35%. The price paid by the customer will vary based on how many licenses they commit to buy. Once your contributor account balance reaches a minimum of $25, you can submit a payment request using PayPal, Skrill, or (in some regions outside the U.S.) Payoneer.

Continue to grow your portfolio and watch your revenue increase. Even while you sleep.

# 20.

# YOUR MONEY CAN WORK HARDER FOR YOU THAN YOU CAN

The year was 1985. Susan and I were night scuba diving along with some friends, off the Kenya coast. Seeing and photographing the underwater wonders of the Indian Ocean was an amazing and memorable experience.

After the dive, standing on the beach and looking up at the stars in wonderment, we were talking with two of our friends, Gus and Jean Gilderbloom. They were in their early 70s; I was 35. We were talking about how lucky we were to be doing what we wanted to do.

"May I give you some advice?" Jean asked.

"Please," I said.

"You are young and have your whole life in front of you. Always remember this: your money can work harder for you than you can."

Jean, who traveled the world with Gus, went on to talk about the importance of saving money and investing wisely. "It's the key to keep doing what you want to do," she said.

I have always kept Jean's advice in mind, working hard for, and saving, those "peanuts" that my dad talked about. Susan and I have also lived below our means and have made investing a priority.

I really can't give you any solid financial advice because I am not a financial expert. One suggestion, however, is that it's important to seek financial advice: find an accountant, financial advisor, or wealth manager if you "want to do what you want to do in life," especially as you get older.

Your financial advisor *may* suggest (as I suggested earlier in this book about your photography business): "Don't put all your eggs in one basket." In other words, diversify your investments as well as your photo skills.

One more tip: If you can, it's probably best to wait until you are seventy to collect social security. The payout at sixty-five is substantially lower than it is at seventy. Hey, if you're in your thirties or forties, that may seem like a long way away. All I can say, my friend, is this: don't blink.

I do, however, know someone who can give financial advice. He's my good friend, excellent photographer, and a wealth advisor at a major Wall Street firm.

The firm' policy does not allow freelance work, so I can't share his name with you. But take it from me, he is one very highly respected wealth advisor.

When I asked my friend to contribute to this book, he enthusiastically agreed, because he is one of the nicest, most caring, and most sharing people I know.

Following are his words of wisdom.

## Money: A Blessing or a Curse?

Money is a topic of discussion that brings up many feelings, emotions, opinions, and satisfaction or frustration. In and of itself money is neither good nor bad. Money is only a tool. It can be used for noble or wasteful purposes. Remember, money isn't the "root of all evil," it's the *love* of money that is the root of all evil. Money can control us, or we can learn to control it.

Whatever our endeavors are, we are going to need to learn to use money to benefit our lives, our family, or it can enslave us and destroy our family, our future, and everything we hope to accomplish in our lives. We live in a society where money is the means of exchange. So, no money, no exchange, no food, no clothes, no housing, no travel, etc. We have to have money to survive, subsist, and flourish. How much is up to you. Last time I checked, Canon, Nikon, and Sony were not willing to barter for their equipment.

After forty-one years as a financial advisor, I have seen both those who are "good with money" and those who never learned to control and manage their financial lives. You have heard people say that a photographer has a "good eye." That does not consider their knowledge, their experience, their discipline, their vision, their following of great photographers (e.g., Rick Sammon), etc. It is the same with money. People are not just good with money, it takes time, knowledge, experience, work with experts, and study to be successful with money. Like almost all good things in our lives, handling our financial lives takes discipline, commitment, and a long-term plan. It takes self-control, focus, and desire.

I have worked with many very wealthy clients and some look at money or their net worth as a score card, to see how much they can run up the score. Other clients have met all their own needs and then accomplished much good with what they have accumulated. Their generosity has helped, blessed, and lifted many others through their support of worthy causes.

I have always loved this Norman MacEwen quote: "We make a living by what we get, we make a life by what we give."

I also like this thought from Franklin Roosevelt: "Happiness lies not in the mere possession of money; it lies in the joy of achievement, in the thrill of creative effort."

So, what are some of the basic principles of financial success? Most are long-term lessons we learn that require discipline and consistency. You will notice that none of these talk about how much money you earn, but what you do with what you earn.

Here are a few to consider:

1) Create and use a budget. Get organized and know your income and expenses. Set some goals and stick to those goals consistently over the long term.

2) Pay down or eliminate debt. Nathan W. Morris said, "Every time you borrow money, you are robbing your future self." Debt should never be permanent; it should be temporary and paid off as quickly as possible. Sometimes you have to borrow money to buy a home or start a business or get an education. But pay it off and finance yourself as you soon as you can. The best leverage is no leverage. The best feeling you can have is to be debt-free.

3) Save some money consistently every month. The first place to save some money is in an "emergency fund." This fund should be four to six months of your monthly living expenses and is used to pay for unexpected costs. This money needs to be safe and liquid and not in your checking account. It can be used for home repairs, car repairs, and medical bills so that you do not have to put those expenditures on a credit card. Rebuild it quickly after using some of it.

4) Save in another account for intermediate term needs for the next five years like a new car, some new equipment, college expenses, or a down payment on a home. The amount in this fund needs to be appropriate to upcoming expenses. While you are saving in this account, it can be invested conservatively for a little higher interest rate. You can have multiple accounts designated for various needs. Again, this will save you from having to borrow money.

5) Save for retirement. While this purpose is often pushed off into the future, this is a mistake. To produce a comfortable retirement, it takes your whole career to save enough; it is not something you can do in the last five years of your career. If you work for an employer that has a retirement plan like a 401k,

absolutely use it, especially if the employer offers a company-paid match. Always save at least up to the level the employer matches. It can be more difficult when you are self-employed but is just as important and takes even more discipline. Set up an IRA, Roth, or retirement plan for the tax benefits and make a rock-solid commitment to contribute to it every year. You can also save for retirement outside of a retirement plan too but invest it suitably for the time frame and the tax issues.

6) Learn to invest appropriately. To earn returns higher than money markets or bank accounts, you have to accept some risk. But that risk can be modest, and in the long run, acceptable. Do not speculate on high-risk or get-rich-quick schemes. If the speculated rate of return seems too good to be true, it probably is not true. With all investments, be aware of the risk, the administrative costs, and tax issues. Also consider the liquidity and penalties if any is withdrawn. Do not let short-term volatility or market swings derail your long-term goals. Be patient and do not let emotions cause you to make short-term decisions. Most of all, get professional help from reputable firms. Professional help is critical for tax, legal, and investment advice.

These steps cannot be taken overnight, but you can get started and be consistent. As you earn more or pay down debt, savings can be increased and diversified. It will be amazing to you how fast savings and investments can grow as you are consistent and committed to your future.

As your financial life is planned, carried out, and goals are met, your reward is freedom—the freedom to buy what you need or want and to travel to places you dreamed about—and the security of not having to worry about your financial future. As that freedom is achieved, the next greatest feeling is to be in a position to support causes and organizations that are doing good and helping others. Money can be a blessing or a curse, it is up to you and how you plan and control your own destiny.

# 21.

# GOOD NIGHT
# AND GOOD LUCK

*"Good night and good luck."*
—EDWARD R. MURROW

This book is dedicated to my dad, Robert M. Sammon, Senior, who as I previously mentioned, gave me some good business advice (as well as lots of love) when I was growing up.

As an aside, in the 1950s he worked with famed on-air reporter Edward R. Murrow on the CBS television program, *Person to Person*, one of the first live television programs.

At the end of each program, "Murro," as my dad used to call him, always said, "Good night and good luck."

It was that quote that inspired the final chapter in this book.

I hope you now have some ideas on how to make some money while you are sleeping after you have put in the hard work to generate products and services to put on your website (your store) and other places online.

Before I say, "good night and good luck," I'd just like you to consider the benefits of getting a good night's sleep, and even taking a nap, because I believe being rested will help you be more productive while you are awake. I'm not an expert on the scientific benefits of sleeping, but I am interested in the topic, so I did a search.

In my search about napping, I came across this interesting fact that I found on WebMD:

> A team of German neuropsychologists found that napping after learning something can make your memory of that information five times better than if you had stayed awake afterward. The researchers say your brain's ability to go into a tranquil state during sleep is linked to your ability to remember. Mandatory naptime at the office? That's just good management.

And when I was searching for the benefits of a good night's sleep, I found the following on sclhealth.com:

> Even though sleep gives your body the rest it needs, your mind is still hard at work. It's actually processing and consolidating your memories from the day. If you don't get enough sleep, who knows where those memories go. Or worse, your mind might actually create false memories.
>
> The bottom line: Sleep is good. And necessary. Roy Kohler, MD, who specializes in sleep medicine at SCL Health in Montana, reaffirms all we know about the benefits of sleep, citing research that shows people who get less sleep tend to be heavier, eat more, have a higher BMI, and are more likely to be diabetic. 'Consistent sleep of seven hours a night is what's recommended

for adults just for daytime functioning—being on task, being alert for the day and being able to concentrate and not be so moody and tired during the day,' says Dr. Kohler.

While there will certainly be ebbs and flows to your sleeping patterns, we hope this is enough evidence to convince you to aim for seven to eight hours a night so your mind and body can fully reap all the benefits.

Need some help counting sheep? Create a nighttime routine to get your mind and body relaxed, maybe try meditating. Oh, and stop looking at your phone or tablet — those social media alerts will all be there in the morning. Sweet dreams!

Although I am not a sleep expert, I am, as Susan Sammon will tell you, an expert on the actual process of power napping. For the past twenty years or so I have taken a power nap just about every day, while at home and while away. When I wake up, I feel refreshed and invigorated.

I also pride myself on getting a good night's sleep, going to bed early, but waking up early, too.

With that, I'll say, "good night and good luck." Pleasant dreams my friends, and I hope all your dreams—of making good photographs and making some extra income—come true.

# 22.

## APPENDIX: E-COMMERCE WEBSITES

Throughout this book I mention several different e-commerce web sites. For easy reference, I have included them all below, plus I have added a few more.

Before choosing a site or sites for e-commerce, take a deep dive into the features, services, customer support, and of course, cost.

- amazon.com
- artstorefronts.com
- buymeacoffee.com
- contentshelf.com
- etsy.com
- e-junkie.com
- facebook.com
- Instagram.com
- ko-fi.com
- linktree.com
- smugmug.com
- squarespace.com

# AUTHOR'S BIO

Believe it or not, before becoming a professional photographer, Rick Sammon spent 10 years (1980–1990) on the Minolta camera account as vice president/group supervisor at Bozell & Jacobs, one of the largest advertising and public relations agencies in the world at that time.

During his time at Bozell & Jacobs, Rick learned about the business side of photography, as well as how to promote Minolta photographers, like The Beatles famed photographer Harry Benson.

Today, Rick still applies, with some updates, many of the same business principles he learned while wearing a three-piece-suit. His business experience, combined with his passion for photography (having photographed in more than 100 countries) and teaching photography, gives Rick a unique vantage point from which to write about the business side of photography.

Since 2003, Rick has been a Canon Explorer of Light, an honor bestowed on a very select group of photographers.

Rick's enthusiasm for digital imaging is contagious. He is a man on a mission—a mission to make digital photography fun, creative, exciting, and rewarding for others.

Rick has published 43 books, *How to Make Money While You are*

*Sleeping*, being his latest. Yes, Rick likes to write! His three recent books, *Photo Therapy Motivation and Wisdom: Discovering the Power of Pictures*; *Photo Quest: Discovering Your Photographic and Artistic Voice*; and *Photo Pursuit: Stories Behind the Photographs*, have all been #1 best sellers on Amazon. Read more about Rick's books here: https://ricksammon.com/ricks-books.

Rick is also the founder of the Photo Therapy Facebook group, a place where photographers can share their work and learn from others.

While Rick describes himself as "evolving," he hesitates to categorize his work. "I'm an A-to-Z type of photographer. I do it all, and I enjoy the freedom of not specializing."

With more than 50 years of experience, this self-taught photographer has many accomplishments—and many more anticipated for the road ahead. As Rick suggests, "When you are through changing, you are through."

If you'd like to see Rick presenting on camera, check out his Kelbyone.com classes, which are packed with hundreds of images from his travels around the world:

*Sammonisms – Speed Learning Advice for Making Awesome Photographs*
*Backyard Bird Photography and Beyond*
*Uncovering the Magic of the Rainforest: Costa Rica*
*Uncovering the Magic of Utah's National and State Parks*
*Uncovering the Magic of Yellowstone and Grand Tetons*
*Improving Your Creative Vision by Getting It Right in Camera*
*The 20 Time-Proven Rules of Composition*
*Rick's Top Tips for Taking Incredible Travel Photos*
*Breathtaking Bird Photography: Pro Settings and Techniques*
*Composition: The Strongest Way of Seeing*
*How to Stay Motivated in Photography*
*Transform Your Home into a Professional Photo Studio – Part I*
*Transform Your Home into a Professional Photo Studio – Part II*
*Capturing the Wild: Safari Photography*

# PLEASE STAY IN TOUCH

I'd love to stay in touch with you, and I hope you can stay in touch with me. It's always fun and satisfying to hear from readers. Here's how to find me:

### MY WEBSITE
www.ricksammon.com

### ON FACEBOOK
https://www.facebook.com/RickSammonPhotography

### MY PHOTO THERAPY FACEBOOK GROUP
http://bit.ly/GrowWithPhotoTherapy

### ON TWITTER
https://twitter.com/ricksammon

### ON INSTAGRAM
https://www.instagram.com/ricksammonphotography/

Made in United States
Troutdale, OR
12/04/2024